D1336891

Amazing Pets

& how to keep them

To Louis and Jasmine,
I hope that you may be awed by the beauty and intricacy
of these amazing pets and enjoy rearing many of them as
I did during my childhood.

Wild Nature Press Ltd
Registered address
7 Sandy Court,
Ashleigh Way,
Plymouth, PL7 5JX.

www.wildnaturepress.com

Published in 2019

A CIP catalogue record for this book is available from the British Library

ISBN 978-1-9995811-1-4

Printed in Slovenia on behalf of Latitude Press Limited

10 9 8 7 6 5 4 3 2 1

The Don Hanson Charitable Foundation sponsored the donation of one copy of this book to
be sent to each of 10,000 primary schools across the UK. Royalties from the sale of this book
supports the Don Hanson Charitable Foundation's ongoing work to inspire children's
interests in learning about nature, science and the conservation of our world.

Amazing Pets

& how to keep them

STEWART McPHERSON

Edited by Graham Smith and Janice Smith

WILD NATURE PRESS

Contents

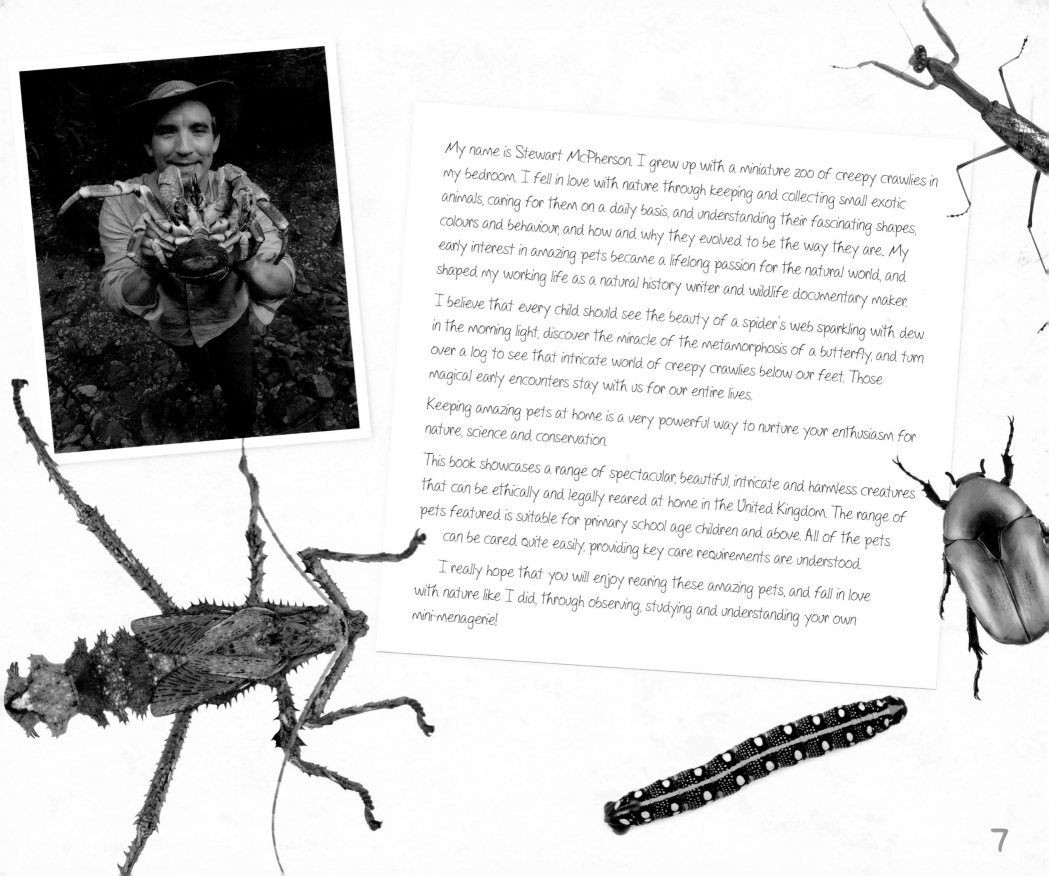

My name is Stewart McPherson. I grew up with a miniature zoo of creepy crawlies in my bedroom. I fell in love with nature through keeping and collecting small exotic animals, caring for them on a daily basis, and understanding their fascinating shapes, colours and behaviour, and how and why they evolved to be the way they are. My early interest in amazing pets became a lifelong passion for the natural world, and shaped my working life as a natural history writer and wildlife documentary maker.

I believe that every child should see the beauty of a spider's web sparkling with dew in the morning light, discover the miracle of the metamorphosis of a butterfly, and turn over a log to see that intricate world of creepy crawlies below our feet. Those magical early encounters stay with us for our entire lives.

Keeping amazing pets at home is a very powerful way to nurture your enthusiasm for nature, science and conservation.

This book showcases a range of spectacular, beautiful, intricate and harmless creatures that can be ethically and legally reared at home in the United Kingdom. The range of pets featured is suitable for primary school age children and above. All of the pets can be cared quite easily, providing key care requirements are understood.

I really hope that you will enjoy rearing these amazing pets, and fall in love with nature like I did, through observing, studying and understanding your own mini-menagerie!

Golden rules

Before you take on a new pet, it is important to understand its needs. This includes learning about how and what it eats and how much and how often to feed it, how it drinks and how much water to provide, the most suitable enclosure to keep it in, and how to provide the right amount of light and heat. You will also need to be aware of how to handle your pet and, if necessary, understand its breeding patterns and behaviours.

Finally, it is important to understand that any pet will make demands of your time on a regular basis, if not daily. This includes feeding, watering and cleaning tasks that might not be your idea of fun. The key thing is to understand that, while pets will bring you endless hours of fascination, there is some hard work involved. But you can be sure that, the greater the effort you make, the healthier and happier your pet will be, making you a whole lot happier too!

THERE ARE FOUR GOLDEN RULES YOU MUST CONSIDER BEFORE CHOOSING A NEW PET:

1 Only ever purchase animals from reputable and ethical sources that are known to look after their animals well.

It can be tempting to go for the cheapest source, or the first supplier that has the animal you are looking for. However it is your responsibility to ensure that your money is going to a supplier that treats their animals well and maintains them in good health, and which does not rely on illegal trade.

Generally, buying animals that are captured from the wild is unethical and unnecessary, since most pets can be bred in captivity with no impact on wild populations. Importing certain wild-caught animals may be banned for fear of introducing disease. For example, wild-caught millipedes can harbour mites that are harmful to agriculture. Always try to source pets from ethical captive breeders.

2 Only obtain animals if you know you can provide suitable conditions for keeping them.

Always research the needs of your prospective pet and compare them with conditions at home. If you live in a cold and draughty home, you will need to provide enclosures with thermostatically controlled heaters for tropical pets. A very warm home might not be suitable for native animals which require a cold winter, unless of course you can provide a safe and sheltered place for them out of doors.

The less you need to modify, the cheaper it will be to keep your pet. It is always best to set up the enclosure properly and test run it for a few days before obtaining your chosen pet, to make sure that everything is working as expected.

In particular, think really carefully about what your pet eats. For example, each species of caterpillar and stick insect eats the leaves of particular types of plants. If the wrong food plant is given, the animals will starve and die. If you cannot supply the correct food, choose a different type of pet!

3 **Only obtain the quantity of animals that you can properly take care of.**

It might seem like a great idea to purchase lots of small animals, but you must ensure that you are able to provide each individual with space and healthy living conditions. The more individuals there are, the more food you must provide, and the more waste you will have to clean up. Of course, some species benefit from company. Talk to your supplier about whether your pet is sociable, and the size of enclosure you should provide.

Also, be very careful handling and holding your pets. Remember, many small creatures are very fragile, and a single drop can cause serious injury or death. Many pets should be handled in a specific way. For example, do not grab a butterfly or moth by its wings, but gently coax it from behind to encourage it to climb carefully onto your outstretched hand.

4 **Never release any animals (or even plants) into the wild.**

Many of the animals that you acquire as pets will not be native to your country. It is important that you never let your pet loose in nature, either on purpose or accidentally. If your pet finds itself alone in the wild, as a captive-raised animal it is likely to lead a short and miserable life out there. More importantly, non-native species can introduce diseases to native wildlife and if the non-native animals survive, they can upset the balance of nature, causing the loss of native wild animals or plants. Non-natives that out-compete native species and become invasive cause environmental catastrophes.

These days, there is an enormous range of fantastically interesting, beautiful and weird animals that can be kept as pets. While many of them have very particular needs that can be difficult for the beginner to provide, there is an equally broad range of animals that are well-suited to being looked after by young people as well as beginners of any age.

The animals featured in this book are those that are safe to rear in your home – most of them are easy to keep, and the few which require a little more care are nonetheless simple in terms of their requirements (such as warm temperatures, or higher humidity levels).

Whichever kind of pet you decide to bring home, most will have the same basic needs. As well as the right enclosure, food, water and temperature, you might need:

- plants or branches for your pet to explore
- a spray bottle/mister to keep humidity levels up
- substrate (such as soil or leaf mould, for example) for the bottom of the tank
- a heating pad (if the temperature in your home is too low).

More specific information can be found in the different animal sections within this book.

Lastly, please note that while all of the animals included in this book may be reared legally in the United Kingdom, certain countries (notably Australia and the United States) have strict rules that prohibit the keeping of non-native species of some animal groups (e.g. stick insects) to prevent the accidental introduction of foreign species. Please contact the local authorities of your country to establish which species you may legally keep at home.

ENCLOSURES

Suitable enclosures will vary depending on the type of animal, but these generally include small glass or plastic fish tanks, large plastic jars with air holes made in their lids, mesh butterfly boxes or purpose-built terrariums. It should have enough ventilation as stagnant air can lead to ill health. Mesh tops are excellent for this, but can reduce humidity, so the choice of lid must be a compromise.

As a general rule, enclosures for land animals should be at least three times as long, wide and high as the maximum length of your pet, but in some cases much larger. A tank of 30cm square is a good size for many smaller animals.

Substrate should be added to the bottom of the tank to a depth of 2cm. An ideal substrate is capable of absorbing water whilst being mould resistant. Suitable examples include soil, peat-free compost, peat-free compost and sand mixes or vermiculite (available at garden centres and some pet shops). Porous substrates like these help to retain moisture and increase humidity.

When cleaning the enclosure, simply remove all substrate and wash the inside of the enclosure with hot water. Do not use any detergent as this can harm some animals. Dry the enclosure and add fresh substrate before returning the animal to its home.

FEEDING

Some pets will eat simple, packaged pellets that can be bought from many pet shops, while others may eat only live insects, fruits or vegetables. You can purchase live foods like crickets or fruit flies from many pet stores.

Always be sure to remove uneaten food from your pet's enclosure to maintain good hygiene.

TEMPERATURES

Keeping tropical species in temperate areas such as Europe and North America may require artificial heating in order to maintain suitable temperatures, especially during winter. This can easily be achieved by using a heat pad suitable for exotic pets. If using a heater, you will need to make sure any substrate does not completely dry out.

WATER

All animals require water, but not all will drink it from a dish! Some insects acquire water only from their food, in which case food must always be fresh and juicy, rather than dried out. Others will drink, but only from tiny droplets on leaves or the walls of the enclosure, in which case the tank and any plants or branches inside should be lightly sprayed every day.

Amazing pets

All the animals included in this book belong to a group of animals called invertebrates.

So, what is an invertebrate?

Invertebrates are animals that do not have a backbone. They are a very large and varied group of creatures. Some, such as earthworms, jellyfish, sea anemones and snails, have soft bodies. Others such as insects, spiders and millipedes, have a hard outer casing (called an exoskeleton) instead of bones inside their body. This outer casing protects them a bit like a suit of armour.

Many invertebrates are small, inconspicuous and little studied, so it is not known precisely how many species of invertebrates exist. What we do know is that there are at least 1,250,000 species, which is most of all animal species on Earth. Each year, thousands of new invertebrates are discovered, and some scientists think that there could be as many as 10 million further species yet to be found! This might seem hard to believe, but many are tiny (or even microscopic) and they often live in very difficult places to reach, such as the canopy of the Brazilian rainforest or the deep sea. As we slowly explore these habitats, amazing discoveries are made. Several hundred (mainly tiny) new invertebrates can be found in just a single tree!

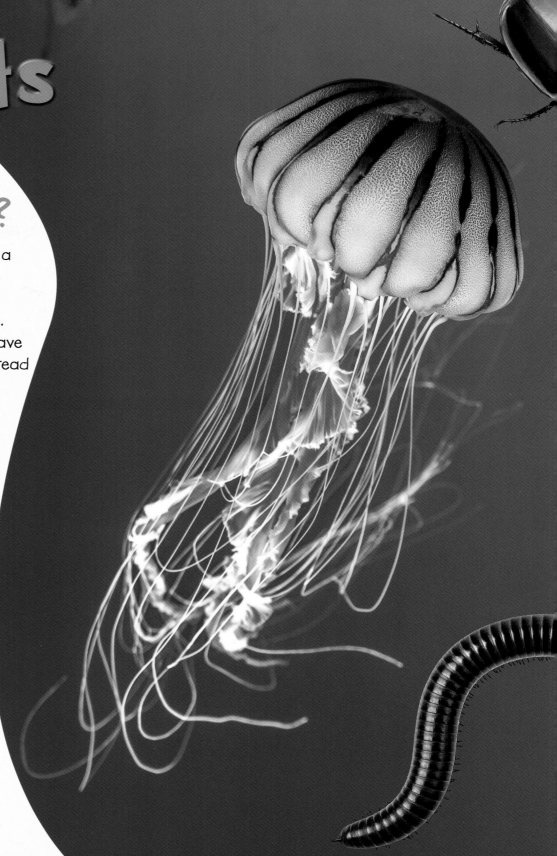

Invertebrates are incredible! They were the first animals to evolve on Earth, and the first animals to emerge from the seas onto dry land. The very oldest invertebrate fossils are dated to 665 million years ago, but some scientists believe they originated much earlier, possibly as early as a billion years ago! Some invertebrates are regarded as 'living fossils' as they have hardly changed for tens of millions of years, such as triops (which you can keep as pets at home – see the triops chapter on page 104).

INVERTEBRATES RULE!

Think about animals... what do you think of? Lions, tigers and elephants? These might be some of the biggest and most impressive animals, but did you know, if you added up all of the invertebrates of the world, their weight would be bigger than all other animal groups combined! It is estimated that there are over 10,000 trillion ants alone, weighing over 40 billion kg!

Let's explore invertebrates further

The two largest groups of invertebrates are the arthropods and the molluscs. We'll look first at the biggest group.

What is an arthropod?

Arthropods have an external skeleton (an exoskeleton), a body that is divided into segments and paired jointed appendages (such as antennae, mouthparts, gills, legs and parts of the tail). Some arthropods have larvae that appear soft bodied, but the adults are all hard bodied, like butterflies and beetles.

Arthropods come in all shapes and sizes, from minute to quite large. They are the majority of invertebrate species, about 80% of all known animal species on Earth, but scientists think many millions of unknown arthropods await discovery.

Incredibly, arthropods live in almost all corners of the globe. There are many types of arthropods, and here we'll just look at the larger groups.

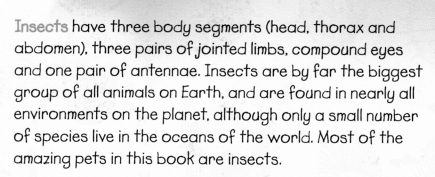

Insects have three body segments (head, thorax and abdomen), three pairs of jointed limbs, compound eyes and one pair of antennae. Insects are by far the biggest group of all animals on Earth, and are found in nearly all environments on the planet, although only a small number of species live in the oceans of the world. Most of the amazing pets in this book are insects.

Crustaceans have hard exoskeletons, pairs of (often highly modified) appendages or limbs and two pairs of antennae. Crustaceans are incredibly varied and include crabs, lobsters, shrimp and even krill, woodlice, and barnacles! Most crustacean species live in aquatic environments (mainly marine), but some also live on land. You can learn about keeping the crustacean triops on page 104.

Myriapods have a single pair of antennae and elongated bodies with numerous leg-bearing segments, such as centipedes and millipedes. Myriapods can often have several hundred pairs of legs! You can find all about the giant millipedes on page 92.

Chelicerates have segmented bodies and jointed limbs and are the only arthropods not to have antennae. They are an ancient group of arthropods and include arachnids (spiders, mites and scorpions), horseshoe crabs and sea spiders.

GROWING PAINS

All arthropods have a hard and non-living exoskeleton which cannot enlarge as the animal grows. Therefore they need to shed it every so often, a process called moulting, in order to increase in size. When an arthropod moults, its exoskeleton splits, and the animal wiggles and climbs out of the old skin. It is now able to expand to a larger size before its new exoskeleton hardens.

What is a mollusc?

All mollusc bodies are soft and unsegmented, most having hard protective shells. They also have a mantle, which is a special body wall that protects their organs. Many molluscs have a specialised tongue called a radula, which acts like a miniature cheese grater used for scraping or cutting food.

Molluscs are the second largest group of invertebrates and about 80,000 species are known today.

There are many types of molluscs including snails and slugs, clams, cockles, mussels, squid, cuttlefish and octopuses. It is astounding to think that the highly intelligent octopuses are related to the simple cockle. Some octopuses have the ability to solve simple puzzles, such as unscrewing jar lids in order to obtain food. Many cases have been recorded in aquariums of captive octopuses climbing out of their tanks during the night, crawling many metres across the ground to reach other tanks of marine creatures, which they enter, to eat up all they can find, before returning to the tank they came from!

Many molluscs have amazing abilities to change the colour of their bodies, either to communicate or to display warning signs. This ability is most highly developed in squid, cuttlefish and octopuses, and some species can completely change colour in the blink of an eye! Their skin contains many thousands of specialised cells called chromatophores. The centre of each chromatophore contains a sac full of pigment like a tiny balloon. This sac can be expanded, making the colour more visible on the animal's skin. That's how these animals can produce amazing displays, often in many different colours.

While many molluscs are tiny, some marine mollusc species grow to gigantic sizes. The Giant Squid can grow to 13m long and weigh nearly a ton, and the little-known colossal squid may grow even larger, and reach up to 14m in length!

One mollusc that makes an amazing pet is the giant land snail, on page 112.

Mantises

Mantises are deadly, nightmarish-looking hunters. They are armed with large claws and are capable of lightning-fast movement. If you were the size of a cricket, they would be the scariest predators you could imagine! The name 'praying mantis' was given to these insects because they hold their front legs up as if in prayer, but this stance is used to ambush prey.

WHAT DOES A MANTIS LOOK LIKE?

The mantis body is composed of the head, the thorax (middle) and the abdomen (rear). All mantises have four walking legs, as well as two front legs that are used to grab prey. These legs are often covered with spines to help them hold on to their prey. The triangular-shaped head of the mantis is the smallest part of its body, with a very large eye on either side and three smaller eyes between them. This unusual shape can make them look very alien! They have two antennae which sit on top of the head, and powerful mandibles (jaws) below that are used to tear apart their prey.

The abdomen can be quite large, but in many species the entire body is relatively slim, allowing them to move quickly.

Most adult mantises have two pairs of wings – a pair of delicate back wings protected under a pair of heavier front wings, which act like wing cases. In many species of mantis, the males can fly while often the females cannot (as they are larger and heavier). In some mantis species, adults lack wings altogether or are small and functionless. Most mantises are 8–10cm long, but the smallest species is 1cm long and the longest over 20cm from front to back!

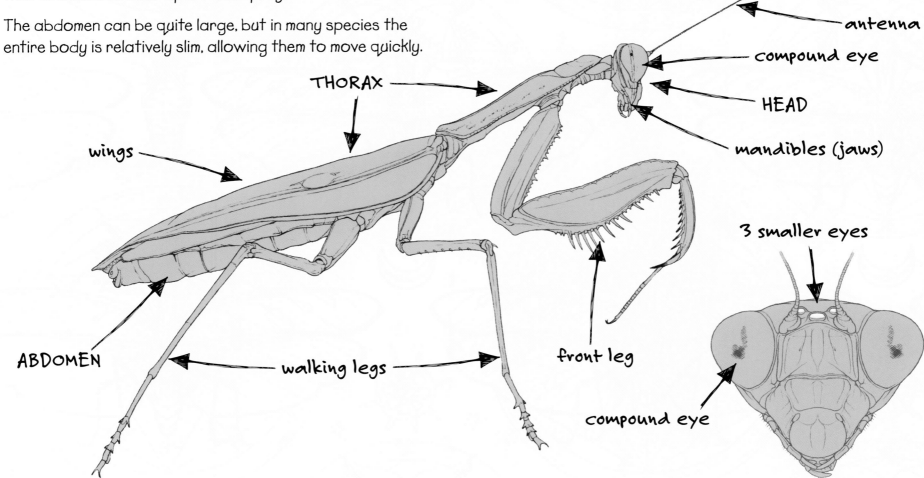

antenna

compound eye

HEAD

mandibles (jaws)

THORAX

wings

ABDOMEN

walking legs

front leg

3 smaller eyes

compound eye

WEAPONRY

Mantises have formidable front legs capable of stretching out and grabbing victims a full body length away. These extraordinary limbs extend and retract in a fraction of a second! They are divided into three parts. The two parts furthest from the mantis's body fold up against each other, like scissor blades. However, they are usually serrated, more like a saw blade, allowing them to pierce the bodies of prey and grip them tightly.

HOW DO MANTISES FEED?

Mantises eat other insects, like butterflies, moths, grasshoppers, crickets, ants, beetles, flies, cockroaches — even other mantises. The largest species in Africa occasionally catch small mice and lizards, while the largest in the Americas may catch small hummingbirds and frogs!

Mantises wait for prey to come to them. Once it's within striking distance, the victim – often as large as the mantis itself – is pulled towards the jaws in an instant. Mantises produce no venom – they simply kill their prey by biting into them while they are still alive. Yum!

DEFENCE BEHAVIOUR

When threatened, mantises may raise their front wings dramatically to reveal striking warning colours. These may startle would-be predators and drive them away. Some species even have expanded front legs bearing bands of colour which they display by rearing up and waving conspicuously.

MASTERS OF DISGUISE

Mantises are ambush predators and rely on camouflage to hide themselves. Most species more or less match their surroundings, with greens and browns being the most common colours, but some mantises look like bright flowers!

Mantis threat displays are often impressive! Some mantis species display their warnings very readily – including even when you walk past their enclosure!

WHERE ARE MANTISES FOUND?

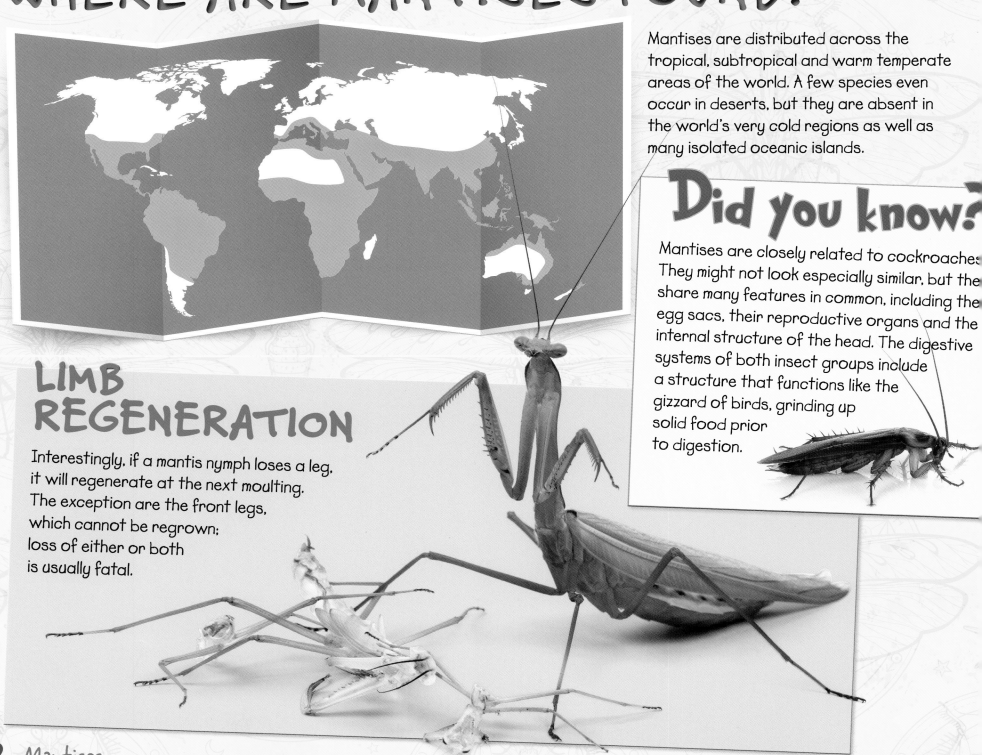

Mantises are distributed across the tropical, subtropical and warm temperate areas of the world. A few species even occur in deserts, but they are absent in the world's very cold regions as well as many isolated oceanic islands.

Did you know?

Mantises are closely related to cockroaches. They might not look especially similar, but they share many features in common, including their egg sacs, their reproductive organs and the internal structure of the head. The digestive systems of both insect groups include a structure that functions like the gizzard of birds, grinding up solid food prior to digestion.

LIMB REGENERATION

Interestingly, if a mantis nymph loses a leg, it will regenerate at the next moulting. The exception are the front legs, which cannot be regrown: loss of either or both is usually fatal.

LIFE CYCLE OF A MANTIS

Mantises can live for six months to one year. There are three stages in their life cycle: the egg, the nymph and the adult.

A mated female will lay an egg sac (an ootheca) on grasses, bushes or twigs within two weeks of mating. This emerges as a frothy mass that soon hardens, providing insulation, protection and camouflage. Its shape and size is unique to each species. The sac contains a separate space for every one of the 200–400 eggs that it contains. In seasonally cold areas, egg sacs are laid in autumn and overwinter till spring, whereas in tropical areas they are laid and hatch at any time. When baby mantises hatch from their eggs as nymphs, they are just 2–7mm long but look like miniature adults, minus wings and adult coloration. Nymphs of some species are camouflaged and may even mimic ants. The nymphs hunt tiny flies, gnats and mosquitoes, but many will try to eat their siblings if food is scarce. Only a few will survive to adulthood.

The predatory nymphs quickly grow, shedding their skins six to nine times before reaching adulthood. To shed, they hang upside down before climbing out of their old skin once it splits open. The new skin is soft at first and expands before hardening. After the final shedding, mantises emerge as sexually mature adults, ready to mate. Despite popular belief, female mantises do not eat the males after biting off their heads. In most cases, the males come away unharmed after mating, less than 30% of the time is he killed and consumed.

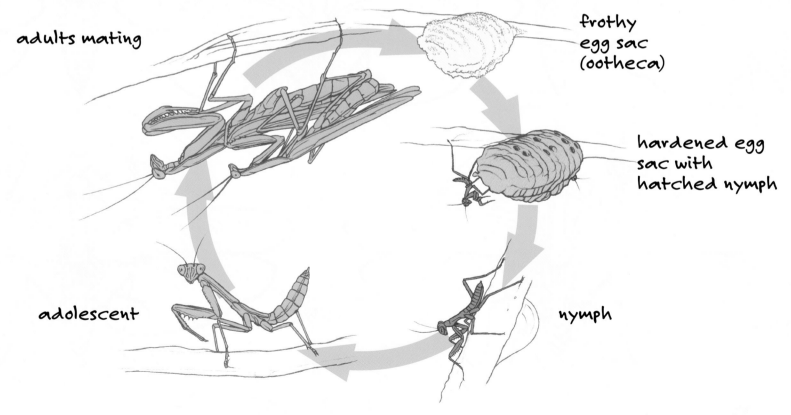

adults mating

frothy
egg sac
(ootheca)

hardened egg
sac with
hatched nymph

adolescent

nymph

RECOMMENDED MANTISES

More than 2,400 species of mantis have been discovered worldwide. The winner for the title of largest mantis is uncertain, but some of the heaviest include species in the Southeast Asian genus *Rhombodera*, while the longest include the *Stagmatoptera* of South America. The smallest mantis known is probably the Australian endemic ground mantis *Bolbe pygmaea*. The adults are only 10mm long and the eyes are only 2mm apart. Mantises make amazing pets, as they have evolved into every imaginable shape and colour to fill the role of predator. The following are among those available as pets.

THE PRAYING MANTIS (*Mantis religiosa*) was the first mantis species to be named and is in many ways the archetypal mantis – green, winged, and holding its front legs up in the typical prayer position.

Florida Bark Mantis – *Gonatista grisea* (adult female)

Praying Mantis

However, there are many species that depart from this general look in weird and wonderful ways. For example, the tiny **BARK MANTISES** have squat, flat bodies, small front legs and mottled coloration just like the bark of trees. Bark mantises wait in ambush to snare other small insects moving up and down their host tree's trunk. Some are so perfectly camouflaged that they appear almost invisible.

Stick mantis - Toxedera sp.

STICK MANTISES, as their name suggests, have very slender, elongated bodies and hide amongst sticks, twigs or blades of grass for camouflage. Their front legs are often very narrow and comparatively delicate, so tend to capture mainly small prey.

Stick mantis - Empusa pennata (nymph)

Grass mantis - Schizocephala bicornis (nymph)

GRASS MANTISES have even better hunting camouflage than stick mantises. Their bodies are extremely long and very thin, and usually they are green, exactly like blades of grass. Their front legs are very long, but have tiny claws, and so they mostly catch small, grass-dwelling flies, gnats and other easy-to-subdue prey!

Boxer mantis - Hestiasula sp. (nymph)

DEAD LEAF MANTISES are the camouflage ninjas. Their unusual wing cases wrap around the abdomen and bear veins, just like a curled up dead leaf, while the thorax is expanded at the sides into the shape of another dead leaf, complete with veins and midrib. The entire body of a dead leaf mantis is brown and occasionally mottled or blemished to look even more convincing. They can have very powerful front legs with dagger-like spines along them, while some species have very dramatically coloured hind legs; when they rear up in a warning display they can appear truly alarming!

BOXER MANTISES are stout insects with massively expanded, very powerful front legs that are capable of grabbing and securing prey animals larger than themselves. The front leg claws of boxer mantises often bear large spines that help them to ensnare their victims. When communicating with each other, these mantises move like boxers in a ring, weaving their front legs in the air, hence their name.

Boxer mantis - Hestiasula sp.

Dead leaf mantis - Deroplatys truncata

Green leaf mantis
Choeradodis stalii (male)

GREEN LEAF MANTISES are similar to dead leaf mantises, but resemble living leaves rather than dead ones. The majority of leaf mantises are bright green, usually with broader abdomens than those of dead leaf mantises, probably because living leaves are more likely to be flattened than curled up. Green leaf mantises also bear veins that resemble those of living leaves.

Green leaf mantis
Choeradodis rhombifolia (female)

Violin mantis – *Gongylus gongylodes* (males)

There is only one species of **GHOST MANTIS** (*Phyllocrania paradoxa*), which is small (up to 5cm) and has a remarkable body structure with many flanges and projections (including a large, asymmetrical structure on the head). The flanges and projections distort the outline of the body so that it resembles a withered leaf. Ghost mantises have very variable coloration. An individual's colour may change each time the skin is shed, and is also dependent upon humidity levels. This species is known as the Ghost Mantis because its camouflage is so perfect that it virtually disappears when motionless!

Ghost mantis – *Phyllocrania paradoxa*

VIOLIN MANTISES are so-named because of their remarkably long, narrow thoraxes rather like the neck of a violin. With the expanded flanges at the top of their thoraxes, their broad forewings and relatively large, pointed antennae, these mantises are very striking indeed!

ROTATING HEADS?

Mantises have incredible eyes and can turn their triangular heads by more than 180°. As a result, mantises can see in almost any direction and can detect prey from a distance of up to 20 metres.

Orchid mantis
Parymenopus davisoni

ORCHID MANTISES take the art of mimicry to the highest level: depending upon the species, they develop white, yellow or bright pink colours on their extremities, while their four walking legs form flattened flanges that resemble petals. Remarkably, these mantises do not camouflage themselves amongst flowers (as is often claimed), but rather, they attract pollinating insects directly, by reflecting ultraviolet light just like real flowers! Sitting on the stems of plants with their whole body arranged to resemble a flower, they simply pounce when insects are drawn to them. Scientists have shown that insects will approach these mantises more often than they do nearby real flowers! Of the several species that can be kept *Hymenopus coronatus* is the most widely available.

Orchid mantis
Hymenopus coronatus

Flower mantis
Creobroter sp.

FLOWER MANTISES

Like the orchid mantis, other mantises rely on bright colours and ultraviolet reflection patterns not to blend in, but to stand out and thereby attract prey. The flower mantises are a broad group of approximately a dozen species, many of which are bright coloured, or have striking patterns in greens, whites and blues across their bodies.

Some species of mantis have eye patterns on their forewings to confuse potential predators. By raising them in display, the mantises may appear larger than they actually are. Used along with warning colours, these tactics are remarkably effective in safeguarding these insects from harm.

Suitable enclosures

Small fish tanks made of glass or plastic, large plastic jars, collapsible mesh butterfly boxes and terrariums can all be used to home an adult mantis. All enclosures must have some ventilation. Use a mesh top or make sure there are number of small holes in the top and sides of the enclosure.

The size of the enclosure is important. It should be at least three times as long, wide and high as the length of your mantis. This will ensure that the mantis has plenty of space to move around in. A 30cm square tank is a good size for most praying mantises. It is important that the container is not too small – if a lack of space prevents the mantis from shedding its skin properly, it may encounter difficulties and die.

HOW TO KEEP A MANTIS

Many species of mantis are relatively easy to keep, allowing us to observe their fascinating behaviour up close. To keep a mantis, you need the following pieces of equipment:

1 An enclosure about 30cm long, wide and tall is ideal

2 Some potting soil for the bottom of the tank

3 Twigs or foliage for use as a perch

4 A spray bottle/mister

5 A heating pad with a thermostat to control temperatures

6 Live insects to be provided as food (these are sold by pet shops).

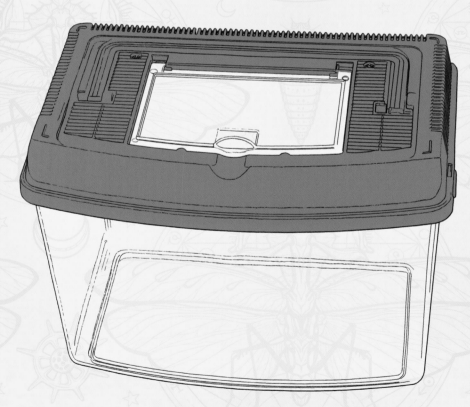

A suitable mantis enclosure

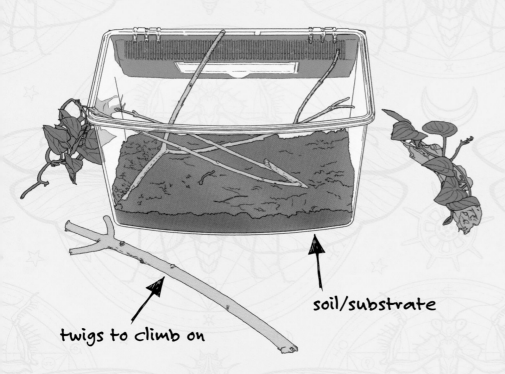

twigs to climb on

soil/substrate

Setting up your mantis enclosure

Soil for enclosure

The bottom of the tank should be filled to a depth of 2cm with potting soil or vermiculite – both can be found at garden centres and even some supermarkets. An ideal base is one that is capable of absorbing water whilst being mould resistant. Porous substrates like soil help to retain moisture and increase humidity, which is particularly important when mantises shed their skins.

Perches

A good perch is also important for shedding, as well as for hunting. You should provide several twigs that reach almost to the top of the enclosure, offering the mantises points from which they can hang. Everything added to the enclosure should be free of insecticides. You can use either living or artificial plants, but the space should not become too crowded.

Cannibals!

All but very young mantises should be kept alone. Mantises will attack and eat other mantises, even their siblings, especially if housed in a small tank!

Cleaning

Since mantises do not produce much waste, their enclosures will not require frequent cleaning. However, the remains of any half-eaten prey must be removed to prevent them from rotting and causing disease. To clean the enclosure, carefully transfer your mantis to a secure container, remove all the soil and then wash the inside with hot water. Do not use any detergents, as some of these can harm mantises. Dry the enclosure and add fresh substrate before returning the mantis to its home.

Water

You do not need to put a water bowl in the enclosure with your mantis. Instead, lightly spray the inside of the enclosure a few times each week. The mantis will drink from droplets that collect on the leaves and twigs, or even the tank wall. Any excess water will evaporate. It is fine for your mantis to become slightly wet, but it should never be drenched, as this sort of treatment could overwhelm it.

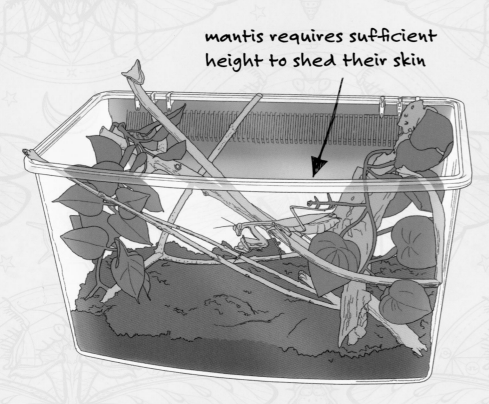

mantis requires sufficient height to shed their skin

A completed mantis enclosure

Other requirements

Most mantises like warm conditions, from 20°C to 28°C during the day and slightly cooler at night. This can be provided by a thermostatically controlled heat pad if you live in a cool climate. If you use a heater, make sure the soil never completely dries out.

If you notice that your mantis has not eaten for several days, it may be about to shed its skin. As the mantis prepares to moult, it is important that it is not disturbed or handled, as this can cause it to fall fatally. By ensuring slightly higher than normal levels of humidity, you will help the mantis to moult without injury.

When your mantis does shed its skin, its new skin will be soft for several hours afterwards. It can easily be damaged at this time and the mantis should be left alone. The new skin will harden within a few hours and the mantis will start to move around its enclosure once more.

Feeding your mantis

Mantises only eat live insects. You can purchase live crickets, locusts and fruit flies from many pet stores.

Mantis prey should always be smaller than the mantis itself. Place one or two prey insects in the enclosure with your mantis every second day. It will generally hunt a new insect every one to four days. Dead or uneaten insects should be removed after a few hours and replaced at the next feeding. Prey animals can simply be placed inside the enclosure for the mantis to find itself, but some people prefer to hold the prey close to the mantis using tweezers. Hatchling mantises require very small prey, cultures of fruit flies are suitable food for these tiny insects.

Holding your mantis

Mantises appear quite delicate, but they can be held and closely observed more easily than many insects. Be aware that mantises may occasionally strike at human fingers with their front legs, but they are unlikely to cause harm and are not venomous. Strikes are generally rare and mantises will only attack fingers if they are waving around like a prey item. Your mantis is less likely to attack fingers that are held flat.

If you wish to hold your mantis, slowly slide your hand under it from the front and let it crawl on. You can gently coax it from behind if absolutely necessary. Do not make any quick motions or grab the mantis from above as this can stress it and cause it to flee, possibly resulting in harm to the mantis.

Allow the mantis to walk across your hand and, when it reaches the end of your hand, put another hand in front of it for it to step onto.

If a female mantis is about to produce eggs, she may have a considerably increased appetite. You will need to provide her with extra food if necessary.

Always be sure to remove dead or partly eaten prey from the enclosure to maintain good hygiene. Make sure that live prey is not hiding or too difficult for your mantis to find, particularly when mantises are young.

Mating pair, note the female is much larger than the male

Breeding mantises

Adult male and female mantises will readily breed when placed together. You can easily tell them apart by studying them from below: male mantises have eight segments to their abdomen while the females have only six. In some species, males and females also look quite different. Mating will usually take place about two weeks after they have shed their skins for the final time.

How to tell male and female mantises apart

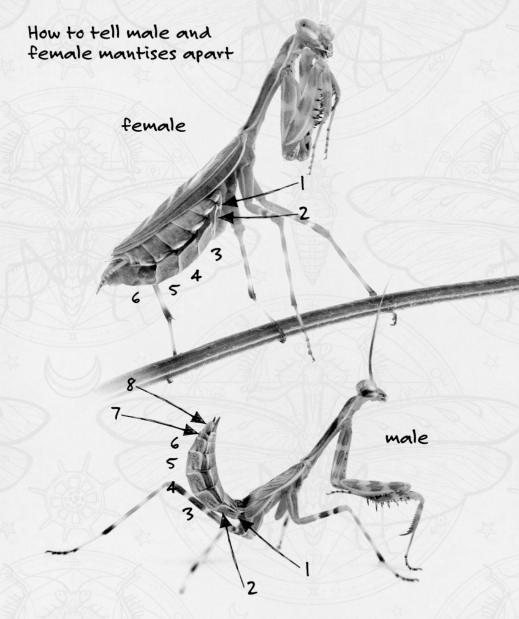

Egg sacs should be kept in an enclosure without large ventilation holes. This is because mantis nymphs are just 2–7mm long and could easily escape through even small holes. Most breeders keep the babies together for a few weeks after hatching. To feed them, provide plenty of fruit flies – wingless varieties are best. Make sure food is always available. Cannibalism is natural for mantises, and if kept together for a long time, the nymphs will feed on each other until a single large nymph remains.

A suitable enclosure for keeping mantis nymphs

In order for your mantises to breed, they will need to be housed in the same enclosure. Before bringing the male and female together, it is important to feed both of them generously. This is to reduce the chances of them eating each other! The enclosure should be the largest that you can provide. Place the pair together in the early evening and monitor the female to ensure that she is not behaving aggressively towards the male. If she seems ready to strike the male, or if the male is agitated, remove one of the two and try again on a different occasion.

If there are no warning signs, the male and female can be left together to mate. This involves the male mounting the female. Mating may take some hours and, in some species, only takes place at night. Once they have mated, the pair should be separated. A successfully mated female will remain fertile for her entire life and does not need to mate again. However, if she lays many egg sacs, it can be wise to allow her to mate again.

Mantis nymphs emerge from an egg sac (oothecal)

Stick Insects

Stick insects are nature's masters of disguise. They are also known as 'phasmids', a name from the Greek word phasma, which means 'ghost'. They were given this name because the insects' camouflage is so remarkably effective that they seem to disappear amongst sticks and leaves like phantoms. One group of phasmids, called leaf insects because they look just like leaves (left), confused early explorers. They thought that the leaves of certain trees came to life when they fell and then wandered off!

WHAT DOES A STICK INSECT LOOK LIKE?

Stick and leaf insects come in a wide number of different shapes, sizes and colours. In some, the males and females look the same, while in others the two sexes look completely different. The smallest stick insects are just 2–3 centimetres long, while the largest may reach up to 62.4cm in length. That record is held by a species found in China, which is the longest insect in the world!

The body of all stick insects is composed of the head, the thorax (middle) and the abdomen (rear). The bulk of the body is made up of the abdomen, which can be large, but is often quite long and thin. All stick insects have six legs, a head, two eyes (as well as additional light-sensitive organs in some species), two narrow antennae and mandibles (jaws) for chewing foliage. Some species have wings, others have only remnants of wings, while some have no wings at all. In winged phasmids, wings develop only when adulthood is reached. The front pair of wings are usually thickened and hard to protect the back pair, a bit like in beetles which have protective wing cases to protect their delicate wings. The protective front wings can be highly camouflaged, with veins, shapes and colours that resemble leaves and bark.

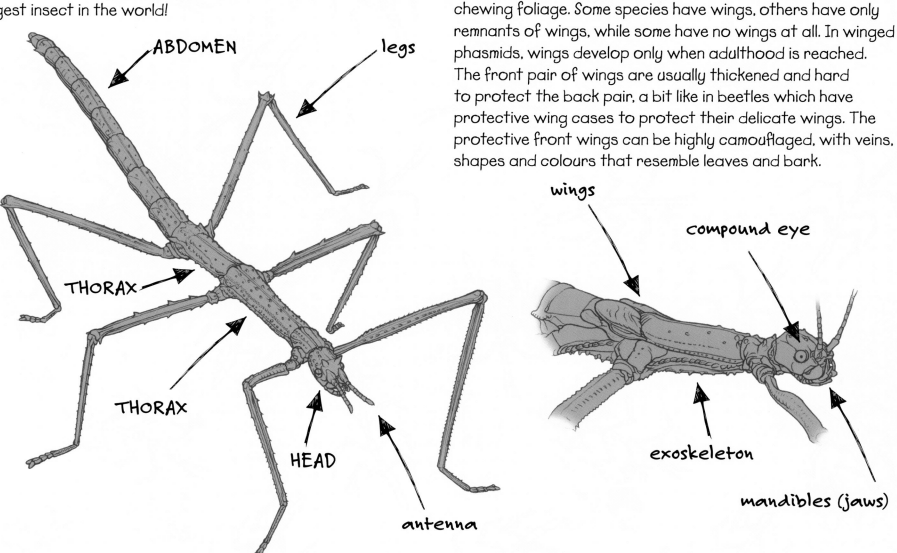

ABDOMEN

legs

THORAX

THORAX

HEAD

antenna

wings

compound eye

exoskeleton

mandibles (jaws)

WEAPONRY

Most stick insects possess no forms of weaponry; however, a number of species have spines on their legs and bodies. The largest of these species have sharp spines on their back legs which they snap together in a pincer-like movement. Others release foul-smelling liquids or irritants to drive back predators.

FAKING DEATH

Some species of stick and leaf insect pretend to be dead when disturbed. Their bodies become rigid, their legs are held along the line of the body and they fall to the ground like leaves or twigs. Finding a camouflaged stick insect amongst leaf litter is extremely difficult!

HOW DO STICK INSECTS FEED?

Stick insects are all herbivores, consuming different types of plant matter, usually leaves. Some species of stick insect eat many different plants, while others will only eat a single plant species.

DEFENCE BEHAVIOUR

Most stick insects rely on extreme camouflage and slow movement to remain undetected by predators. However, when threatened, many will adopt threat displays to try and scare off attackers. This may involve aggressive poses involving bright warning colours, hissing noises made by rubbing their legs together, or the mimicking of scorpions by bending their abdomens forward over their heads.

EXTREME CAMOUFLAGE!

Leaf insects have flattened abdomens and sometimes legs, bearing leaf-like veins and spots, just like the real leaves of plants.

WHERE ARE STICK INSECTS FOUND?

Stick insects are distributed across the tropical, subtropical and warm temperate areas of the world. The majority live in the tropics, where the greatest diversity of species is found.

Different species of stick insects are specialised to living in different layers of vegetation.

CANOPY LEVEL

Many species of stick insects live in the canopy (top branches and leaves) of forests and tend to be really well camouflaged to avoid being spotted by birds, as well as a wide range of other predators. These canopy dwellers include leaf insects, and many long, thin stick insect species, which can hide very effectively amongst the twigs and foliage.

MID LEVEL

Stick insects that live at the mid level of forests tend to be stockier, with a wide range of body shapes, sizes and colours. Many mid-level forest stick insects have mottled green and brown coloration, allowing them to blend in with lichen and moss on bark and branches. They usually have fully functional wings, which allow them to fly between trees when in search of a mate.

GROUND LEVEL

A small number of stick insects are adapted to living mainly at the ground level of forests. These tend to be big, heavy, dark coloured and armoured. They may even have sharp spines to protect them from enemies on the forest floor. Some lay their eggs in soil using an ovipositor (a specialised spike on the female's abdomen which allows eggs to be injected into the earth).

LIFE CYCLE OF A STICK INSECT

Stick insects can live from a few months to about five years, depending on the species. There are three stages in their life cycle: the egg, the nymph and the adult.

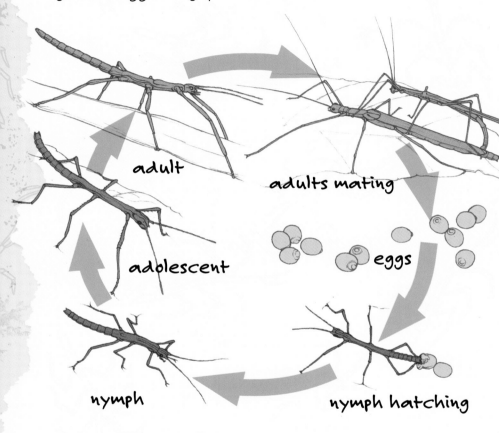

adult

adults mating

adolescent

eggs

nymph

nymph hatching

Stick insect eggs take two to 14 months to hatch, but most species in captivity will hatch in two to four months. The baby insects are very delicate, but look like perfect miniatures of the adults, minus wings and adult coloration. Once hatched, the nymphs locate a food plant and start to eat, growing relatively quickly. As they grow, nymphs will shed their skins between six and nine times before they reach adulthood. Depending upon the species, this may take between three and nine months.

The process of skin shedding is fascinating. A new skin forms under the old one. When ready, the stick insect hangs from a branch and a split develops along the back of the old skin. The moulting insect pulls its body and legs out of the old skin as it slowly extracts itself completely. The new skin is soft but in a matter of hours, the body and legs expand and harden.

Many species of stick insects can reproduce without mating. An unmated female stick insect will only produce eggs that hatch as females, however a mated female stick insect will produces eggs that yield both males and females (although in some species, males are extremely rare or practically absent).

Eggs are either dropped on the ground, buried or glued to bark or the branches of plants. Once they have been laid, the eggs are abandoned by their mother.

Adult females are usually larger than males of the same species, and they often live for longer.

stick insects eggs

RECOMMENDED STICK INSECTS

More than 6,000 species of stick insect have been recorded from around the world. About 300 of those are maintained in captivity, and about 50 are commonly kept as pets. Some of these are relatively easy to look after and make good first-time pets for people new to stick insects.

Annam Stick Insect

Indian Stick Insect

The **ANNAM STICK INSECT** (*Medauroidea extradentata*) from Vietnam is brown to green, up to 14cm long and 9mm wide. This species prefers warmer conditions (18–30°C) in captivity, but happily eats blackberry bramble, hawthorn, oak or rose leaves, making it easy to provide for.

One of the easiest of all stick insects to keep is the **INDIAN STICK INSECT** (*Carausius morosus*). This species comes from Tamil Nadu, a hot southern state of India, yet these insects are rather tolerant of cool temperatures (18–23°C is ideal) and reproduce freely since the females do not need to mate in order to produce eggs. Adult females are olive green to light brown, cylindrical, and up to 10cm long and 6mm wide. They eat privet or ivy leaves and are best first-time stick insects for many people in the UK.

Annam Stick Insects

Giant Prickly Stick Insect

Thorny Stick Insect

One of the most spectacular insects to rear at home is the **GIANT PRICKLY STICK INSECT** (*Extatosoma tiaratum*) from Australia, and it is relatively easy to keep! It is the best non-stick-shaped species of stick-insect for beginners to attempt to rear. Adult females are up to 15.5cm long and 3.5cm wide, making them very robust. They have small wings, small spines and leafy projections along their body. Males are smaller (up to 12.5cm long). They have large, transparent, grey and brown mottled wings and are very capable at flying. Both sexes are variable in colour, but are typically olive green, straw yellow or light brown. The Giant Prickly Stick Insect's preferred food is eucalyptus leaves, but it will also eat the foliage of blackberry bramble, hawthorn, oak, raspberry and rose. This species prefers temperatures of 18–28°C.

THORNY STICK INSECT (*Aretaon asperrimus*) comes from Borneo and is a medium-sized stick insect. Adult females are up to 8cm long, mottled brown and covered with spines. Males are up to 5cm long and more slender but have larger spines on their backs. In both sexes, Thorny Stick Insects are mottled brown. They eat oak, blackberry bramble or rose leaves. Females of these stick insects bury their eggs, so it is important that they have a layer of moist soil or sand in their enclosure. They should be kept at temperatures of 20–28°C and require high levels of humidity.

Jungle Nymph

JUNGLE NYMPH (*Heteropteryx dilatata*) come from the Malay Peninsula and females of this species are among the world's heaviest insects (weighing up to 65g), being up to 25cm long and 7.5cm wide. Their bodies are a vivid shade of lime green and lined with small spines. The males are up to 14cm long, 3cm wide, and mottled brown with a lime green stripe down both sides of the forewings. The males also have plum-purple veined wings and are very capable at flying, unlike the females, which have small display wings. Jungle Nymphs should be kept at temperatures of 20–28°C with high humidity and fed blackberry bramble, raspberry or rose. Females of these stick insects bury their eggs, so it is important that they have a layer of moist soil or sand in their enclosure. When disturbed, both sexes of this species raise their spiny hind legs which they snap closed in a pincer-like movement that can draw blood; adults can nonetheless be held if handled carefully. Allow the insects to walk onto your hand rather than grabbing them, and ensure all hand movements are slow and gentle. This species is one of the longest living of all stick insects and can live up to two years in captivity. This is an incredible insect to rear, but perfect your techniques keeping other stick insect species before attempting to keep this species.

The **BLACK BEAUTY STICK INSECT** (*Peruphasma schultei*) comes from northern Peru and is one of the prettiest species of stick insects in captivity. Both sexes are stocky; the females are up to 55mm long and 7mm wide, whereas the males are up to 43mm long and 5mm wide. Females, males and nymphs are a dusty black colour, with bright yellow or white eyes and red mouth parts. The adults have small black forewings lined with bright white venation. When disturbed, they flash their diminutive, bright crimson wings to startle enemies. This species should be kept at temperatures of 18–28°C and fed privet and honeysuckle leaves.

Note: this species can spray a chemical deterrent from glands behind the head, and this spray can be an irritant, especially if it comes in contact with the handler's eyes.

Giant Spiny Stick Insect

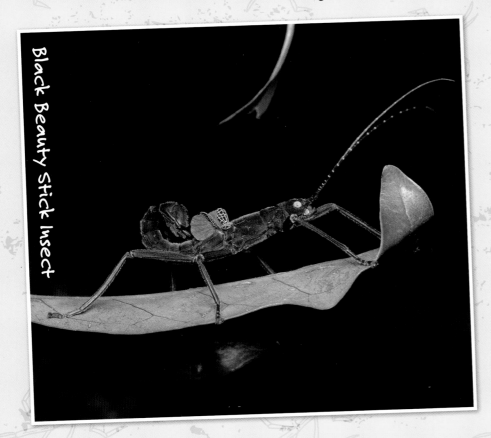

Black Beauty Stick Insect

The **GIANT SPINY STICK INSECT** (*Eurycantha calcarata*) comes from New Guinea, New Caledonia and the Solomon Islands. This species dwells on the forest floor, is wingless, but carries rigid armour and many small spines. Females grow up to 15cm long and 3.5cm wide, whereas males are up to 12cm long and 2.5cm wide. Adults are dark brown to glossy black. The males have enlarged hind legs with a single, massive curved spine on the underneath of each femur (upper leg). When disturbed, both sexes of this species may raise their spiny hind legs and snap them closed in a pincer movement that can draw blood. Adults, but especially males, should be handled carefully. This species should be kept at temperatures of 18–28°C. It requires high levels of humidity and should be fed oak, blackberry bramble, raspberry, rose, ivy or guava leaves. Females of these stick insects bury their eggs, so it is important that they have a layer of moist soil or sand in their enclosure.

PERUVIAN FERN STICK INSECT

(*Oreophoetes peruana*) is amongst the most colourful of all known stick insects. Originating from Peru and Ecuador, their nymphs are black with white stripes along their bodies, a yellow head, yellow knee joints and a yellow tip to their abdomen. Adult females are the same colour, but adult males are bright red, with black stripes along their body and black legs. Males and females grow up to 8cm long and 5mm wide and have very thin legs. This species requires warm temperatures of 22–28°C and high humidity, eating only fern leaves. The foliage of Bird's-nest Ferns (*Asplenium nidus*), bracken (*Pteridium aquilinum*) and many commercially sold fern species are eaten, but be careful not to offer any commercially produced ferns that may contain insecticide.

Giant Green Stick Insect

Peruvian Fern Stick Insect

GIANT GREEN STICK INSECT (*Diapherodes gigantea*) originate from Grenada and several other nearby Caribbean islands. The females of this stick-shaped species grow up to 19cm long and 2.5cm wide, and are vivid green with yellow eyes. The males are up to 11cm long, brown and much thinner than the females, with large brown wings and are capable of flying. Giant Green Stick Insects eat eucalyptus, oak and blackberry bramble leaves. This species should be kept at 20–28°C in very large cages that are at least 60cm tall (hanging butterfly net enclosures work well).

A superficially similar species is the **GOLIATH STICK INSECT** (*Eurycnema goliath*) which originates from Australia, and grows up to 21cm. It has essentially the same growing requirements as the Giant Green Stick Insect, except that it eats eucalyptus and oak leaves.

LEAF INSECTS (*Phyllium bioculatum* and *P. giganteum*) have broad, thin bodies that closely resemble leaves, and legs with expanded flanges. Both of these species are typically green, often with brown blemishes to mimic leaves with amazing accuracy. All male *Phylliym* have wings when mature and can fly well. However, while females do have wings, they are heavy-bodied and flightless. *Phyllium giganteum* originates from the Malay Peninsula and grows up to 15cm long and 4.5cm wide. *Phyllium bioculatum* is distributed from Sri Lanka and Madagascar, across southern Asia to Bali. Females of this species grow up to 10cm long and 3.5cm wide. Leaf insects eat oak and blackberry bramble and require temperatures of 22–30°C (but ideally 25–30°C). Humidity levels of 65–75% are ideal and should not drop below 60%. Leaf insects should be lightly sprayed with chlorine-free water each day (best in the evening); but they should not be drenched, and air movement in their enclosure is needed (sealed tanks with stagnant air generally do not work well). A ventilator is recommended to create a slow, gentle breeze for a few minutes every quarter of an hour to prevent mould from forming in the enclosure, which can result in fatal infections. Leaf insects are more difficult to rear than most stick insects, and keeping them should only be attempted after you have mastered keeping other species.

Phyllium bioculatum

HOW TO KEEP A STICK INSECT

Many species of stick insect are easy to keep in a glass or wire mesh tank. You need the following pieces of equipment:

1 **An enclosure about 30 cm long, wide and tall is ideal, but taller enclosures are even better**

2 **For some species, soil at the bottom of the tank or in a dish will help with egg laying**

3 **Suitable food leaves in a container of water to provide food and a perch**

4 **A spray bottle/mister**

5 **A heating pad with a thermostat to control temperatures for species that like warmer conditions.**

Suitable enclosures

Stick insects can be raised in fish tanks made of glass or plastic, as well as in collapsible mesh butterfly boxes and terrariums. Good vertical height will allow for natural positioning of food plants. All suitable enclosures must have ample ventilation by way of a mesh top or a number of small holes in the top and sides of the enclosure.

As with mantises, the size of the enclosure is important. It should be at least three times as long, wide and high as the length of your stick insect. Since some stick insects can be quite long, it is important to get this right so that the insect has plenty of space to move around in, as well as to shed its skin. If a lack of space prevents the stick insect from shedding its skin properly, it may encounter difficulties and die. Generally speaking, a 30cm square tank is a good size for medium-sized phasmids (species whose adults are 5–13cm long) while a 60cm square tank is sufficient for large species (14–20cm long).

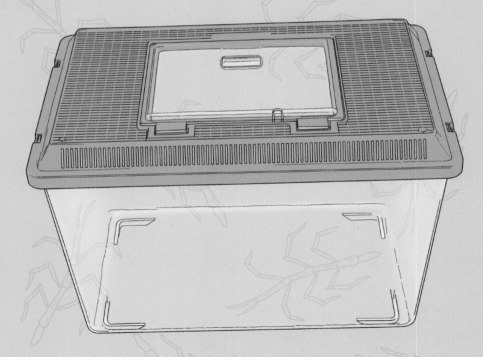

A suitable enclosure for keeping stick insects

Bottom of the enclosure

For many stick insects, it is not necessary to place soil at the base of their enclosure as they do not bury their eggs. For these species, which drop or flick their eggs, it is easiest to place a few sheets of paper inside the enclosure to make cleaning easy. Every week or two, you can lift out the sheet of paper to remove all eggs and droppings, and replace it with a new sheet. Stick insects produce fairly dry waste which is easy to clean up.

For species which inject eggs into the soil, enclosures should have a 5cm layer of soil, or simply a deep dish or container of soil at least 5cm tall. The material in the container can consist of soil, peat free compost or vermiculite (sold at garden centres for plants). Sand often works well and makes it easy to find the usually dark-coloured eggs. The soil should be kept damp but not wet, to stop the eggs from drying out completely.

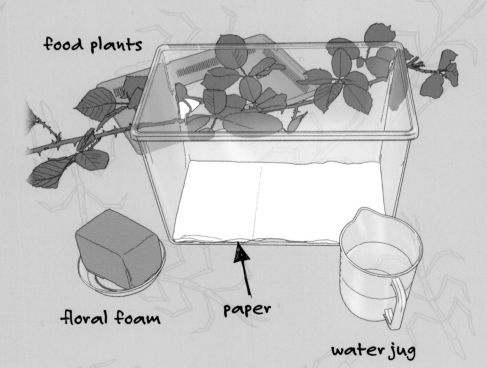

food plants

floral foam

paper

water jug

Setting up a stick insect enclosure

OOPS!

Stick insects are herbivores and can be safely kept together. However, if you ever keep leaf insects, don't house them with stick insects. Leaf insect camouflage is so good that their stick insect cousins sometimes end up chewing on them in the belief that they are plants!

A few species glue eggs to the stems of food plants or to the sides of their enclosure. In these species, the eggs should not be forcibly removed.

Cleaning

Stick insects do not produce much waste, but periodic cleaning is important to prevent diseases. To clean the enclosure, carefully transfer your pets to a secure container, remove everything inside the enclosure and then wash the inside with hot water. Do not use any detergents as some of these can be harmful to insects. Dry the enclosure and replace its contents before placing your stick insects back into their home.

Water

You do not need to put a water bowl in the enclosure with your stick insects. If you lightly spray the inside of the enclosure a few times each week, the stick insects will drink from droplets that collect on leaves, twigs and the tank wall. Any excess water will evaporate. Do not spray insects heavily, although most species will appreciate a light misting.

A fully set up stick insect enclosure

Other requirements

It is easiest to select stick insects that will do well at room temperature in your home. Many species require temperatures of 20–28°C during the day. For these, warmth can be provided by a thermostatically controlled heat pad if you live somewhere with cool weather. If you use a heater, make sure the soil never completely dries out.

Feeding your stick insect

Some stick insects will eat the leaves of particular species of plants. If the incorrect food leaves are provided, the insects will starve and die. Place small branches or sprigs of the leaves of the correct plants in the middle of your stick or leaf insect enclosure in a water-filled container, pot or narrow-necked bottle so that the foliage will remain fresh for several days. Cover the opening of the water container with foil or waterproof paper (you may find an elastic band useful for securing the covering), or plug it with tissue paper to prevent insects from falling inside and drowning. Soaked brick floral foam also works well. Change the food leaves when they begin to discolour, wilt or shrivel.

Where possible, select fresh stems from plants growing away from busy roads or other sources of pollution. Do not feed the insects with plants that have been treated with insecticide, as this will be fatal. Some stick and leaf insect enthusiasts grow food plants as small potted plants and rotate them from being inside in the enclosure to the garden or greenhouse to allow regeneration of leaves.

Most stick and leaf insects can be fed the leaves of many different plant species. Where possible, it is advisable to provide a mixture of suitable plant species to give your pet insects a varied diet.

Containers for food plants

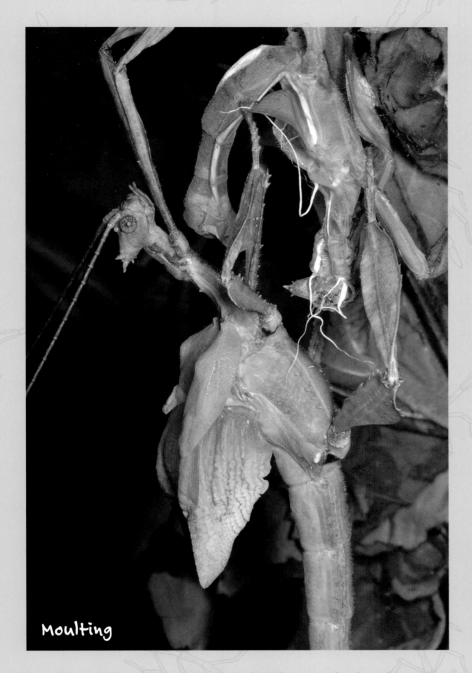

Moulting

A stick insect that stops eating may be about to shed its skin. It is important that it is not disturbed or handled, as this can cause injury. Simply ensure slightly higher than normal levels of humidity and, when it does shed, leave it well alone for several hours – its new skin will be soft and is easily damaged at this time.

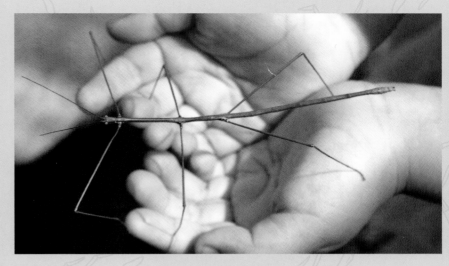

Holding your stick insect

Stick and leaf insects are easy to handle, but many species are fragile and need to be held gently. Do not grab or forcefully pull stick or leaf insects, particularly by the legs, which may detach. Instead, gently grip the body of your pet between your thumb and forefinger to pick it up, or better, allow the insect to walk onto your hand, gently nudging it from behind if necessary. Young animals can be nervous and may drop unexpectedly to the ground, which can result in injury, so it is best to avoid holding pet stick insects in positions where they could fall over long distances.

Mating pair of Peruvian Fern Stick Insects

Breeding stick insects

For those species of stick insects that do not need to mate to reproduce, the females will automatically start laying fertile eggs when they reach adulthood.

For species that can reproduce sexually, it is advisable to allow pairs to mate where possible, as this will result in eggs that hatch faster, producing healthier young. Many species must mate in order for fertile eggs to be laid. Breeding stick and leaf insects is very simple. Simply place adult males and females of the same species together in an enclosure, and the insects will do the rest. Many species remain coupled for extended periods of time, so it is best not to separate them whilst they are paired, as it may result in damage.

Laying eggs

Eggs (above) will be dropped or flicked to the bottom of the enclosure or injected into soil. For eggs that are dropped to the bottom of the enclosure, a sheet of paper can be left there and used to easily remove all of the droppings and eggs. Some stick insects glue their eggs to surfaces (e.g. the side of the enclosure) and should be left to develop where they are. Eggs that have been separated from droppings and substrate should be placed in a small pot and kept on damp, not wet, tissue paper or on muslin cloth. Make sure no mould forms on the eggs or the paper, as this will kill the eggs. Allow the paper to dry up in between misting it with water, to ensure mould cannot take hold. Do not allow the eggs to dry up completely, as this will be fatal. Keep the eggs at 25–28°C. Depending upon the species, the eggs will hatch within a few months.

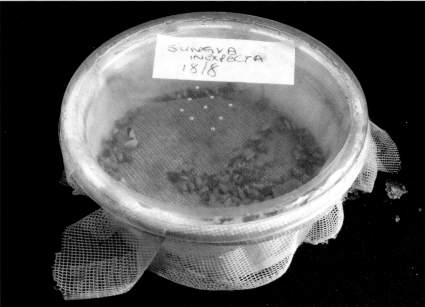

Newly hatched nymph

Newly hatched nymphs (left) tend to emerge during the night and will cluster on the ceiling of the enclosure. Newly hatched nymphs are very fragile and are best moved using the tip of a soft paintbrush, but only if necessary.

Butterflies & moths

Butterflies and moths are some of the most recognisable insects, but did you know that it is possible to raise them in captivity? They are pretty ancient insects – moths appeared 190 million years ago and there are now about 160,000 species worldwide, while butterflies evolved from moths about 55 million years ago, giving rise to about 18,500 species today. The scientific name for the butterfly and moth group is Lepidoptera, which means 'scaled wing'. This refers to the millions of tiny scales on their wings that give them their patterns and colours.

WHAT DO THEY LOOK LIKE?

Butterflies and moths have a head, thorax (middle) and abdomen (rear), with three pairs of legs and two pairs of wings attached to the thorax. Adults possess a long, straw-like proboscis for feeding on nectar from flowers – this is usually coiled up when not in use (see page 56). Their larvae (caterpillars), have no proboscis, but mandibles (jaws) which they use to chew through leaves.

The main difference between butterflies and moths is not obvious – most people think that butterflies are active in the day and that moths only fly at night. However, many moth species fly in the daytime and are very brightly coloured, just like butterflies, so this isn't entirely true. Generally, butterflies have thread-like antennae tipped with tiny clubs and rest with their wings closed together. Moths, on the other hand, have feathery or unclubbed antennae and rest with their wings flat, but there are always exceptions, so you may need to consult an expert to be completely sure!

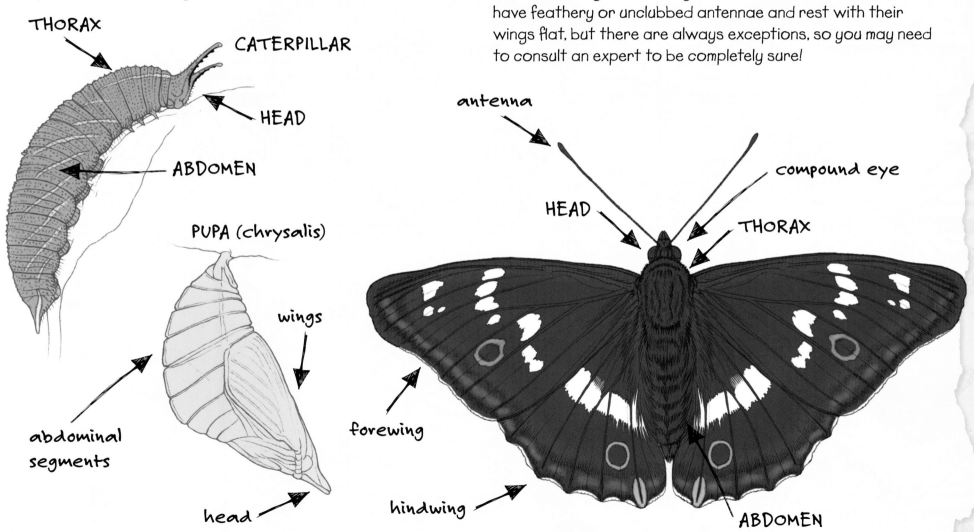

THORAX

CATERPILLAR

HEAD

ABDOMEN

PUPA (chrysalis)

wings

abdominal segments

head

antenna

compound eye

HEAD

THORAX

forewing

hindwing

ABDOMEN

WEAPONRY

The most impressive weapons of butterflies and moths are produced as defences by their caterpillars. Irritating hairs and venomous spines are the most commonly seen and perhaps the most effective. People are warned not to touch hairy caterpillars with good reason – the hairs can cause rashes, or much worse!

A STICKY SITUATION!

Caterpillars of a moth found in Central America are coated in a transparent, gooey layer of jelly. They aren't toxic, but predators can become stuck in this jelly, so they simply avoid eating them!

HOW DO BUTTERFLIES & MOTHS FEED?

Some species do not eat at all as winged adults. Others, which usually survive for longer periods or which migrate over long distances (like the Monarch), typically consume nectar from flowers through their proboscis.

DEFENCE BEHAVIOUR

Caterpillars rely on a number of methods to protect themselves. Some display bright warning colours which suggest that they are poisonous to eat (this can be a bluff), while others produce large eye-spots that make them look like larger animals, or which mimic the head of a snake. A large number of species are highly camouflaged, mimicking twigs or fresh, wet bird droppings, putting off most animals. Tropical leaf-mimic butterflies often remain effectively invisible until they are disturbed. Their resemblance to leaves, may even include veins and fake blemishes.

IS THERE A DEADLY CATERPILLAR?

Yes! The most notorious is the caterpillar of a South American Giant Silkworm Moth (*Lonomia obliqua*). It is responsible for the deaths of about 500 people, mainly men involved in clearing vegetation who simply touched the caterpillars by accident. Toxins (poisons) in the hairs cause internal bleeding that can result in death if not treated in time. Fortunately, most hairy caterpillars are far less dangerous. If in doubt, admire but don't touch!

WHERE ARE BUTTERFLIES & MOTHS FOUND?

Butterflies and moths are found across the world and in almost every type of habitat, the exception being Antarctica. As might be expected, they are most numerous and varied in the tropics. A few species are found in the northern polar region, the caterpillar of the Arctic Woolly Bear (*Gynaephora groenlandica*) pictured can hibernate through winters of -70°C in northern Canada and Greenland. That's cold! With a thick coat of long hairs and blood containing a natural antifreeze, it is one of the toughest insects in the world.

Some butterfly and moth species also occur in extreme desert environments and at high altitudes.

As many butterflies and moth caterpillars only eat certain types of plants (some cases just one type of plant), they are only found where these plants grow. A few eat a wide range of plants and can some of these can reach plague proportions, as millions of hungry caterpillars gobble up human crops or grasslands!

SCALY WINGS

The amazing colours and patterns found on butterfly and moth wings are made of millions of tiny, coloured or light-bending microscopic scales. These scales don't just look beautiful, the patterns and colours are used for mimicry, camouflage and warnings. They also help to insulate the insect. These miniature mosaics make for very delicate wings as the scales can easily be lost – although this can help them escape from spiders' webs!

LIFE CYCLE OF BUTTERFLIES & MOTHS

Both butterflies and moths go through a four-stage life cycle: the egg, the caterpillar (larva), the pupa (chrysalis) and the adult. Eggs are laid on a host plant, and caterpillars hatch out. These feed heavily on the plant and often develop quickly, increasing in size until they are ready to undergo metamorphosis. This is the amazing process by which they change into winged adults!

Caterpillars transform into an adult butterfly or moth inside a chrysalis (pupa). The chrysalis is a layer of hard skin revealed when the caterpillar sheds its skin for the last time. Once exposed, it starts to dry out, becoming stiff and forming a rigid, protective capsule. Some species of moth spin a soft cocoon around themselves before they develop into a chrysalis. Within the chrysalis the caterpillar transforms into an adult (butterfly or moth), before finally emerging.

A butterfly or moth will usually survive for a matter of weeks or months once it has emerged, so it wastes no time in finding a mate. Males often locate females by smell, since the females produce perfumes to reveal where they are. Once a male and female have met, they flutter around each other in a courtship flight, which eventually leads to mating, which occurs tail-to-tail (see page 77). The resulting eggs are laid on the leaves or stems of suitable food plants, and often have a waxy surface that prevents them from drying out.

Eggs hatch within a matter of weeks or months, and the young caterpillars begin to feed almost immediately, starting with their own egg shells. Most caterpillars eat the leaves of their host plants, a few species eat fruit, and even fewer (less than 1% of species) are carnivorous, ambushing other insects or stealing ant eggs for food!

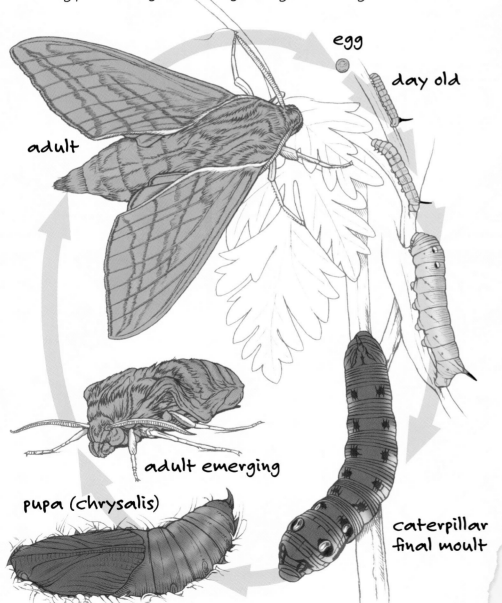

egg

day old

adult

adult emerging

pupa (chrysalis)

caterpillar final moult

RECOMMENDED BUTTERFLIES & MOTHS

All in all, there are more than 178,500 species of butterfly and moth worldwide, but only 10% of all those species are butterflies! Moths reign supreme, but often go unseen because we are much more likely to notice day-flying butterflies.

The **PEACOCK** (*Aglais io*) butterfly is an attractive species, featuring rusty red wings with bright blue eye-spots lined with yellow. The caterpillars of this species eat stinging nettles, which grow widely across Europe and North America. The adult butterflies drink nectar in the wild, and so need to be provided with sugar water and cut soft fruit.

Only a small proportion of the known species of butterflies and moths are kept in captivity, but these are generally both relatively easy to keep and especially beautiful. Many of the most impressive and most suitable butterflies and moths for rearing in captivity are shown over the following pages.

Papilio machaon

The **PURPLE HAIRSTREAK** (*Favonius quercus*) occurs across much of Europe (including the British Isles), North Africa and parts of the Middle East. Males of this species have a glossy purple sheen on the upperside of their wings, while females have two iridescent purple patches on their forewing only. Caterpillars of this butterfly eat the leaves of oak trees (*Quercus cerris, Quercus ilex, Quercus petraea* and *Quercus robur*). Larvae pupate in leaf litter and adults need to be provided with sugar water and flowers to drink nectar from.

SWALLOWTAILS (*Papilio* spp.) are a diverse group of spectacular butterflies with dramatic wing coloration, often in striking patterns of black, light yellow, gold and blue. Each species has its own food requirements, but many swallowtails eat leaves of citrus plants, carrots, parsley, dill, fennel, Queen Anne's Lace (wild carrot) and rue. The caterpillars grow quickly, and may pupate within four weeks, and emerge from their chrysalises within one to two weeks. Adults of most swallowtails require sugar water and cut soft fruit.

The caterpillars of the **MONARCH** (*Danaus plexippus*) butterfly have dramatic yellow, white and black bands along their length, and eat the leaves of milkweed plants (which are easy to grow and have colourful flowers). Caterpillars take just 10-14 days to turn into a butterfly in the chrysalis. Adult have distinctive black, orange and white patterns on their wings. They drink nectar and should be provided with sugar water and cut soft fruit.

The **RED ADMIRAL** (*Vanessa atalanta*) has dark wings, with distinctive bands of orange and white spots. The caterpillars eat the leaves of nettles, and also Hop, Small Nettle and Pellitory-of-the-wall. Red Admiral butterflies drink from rotting fruit, sap oozing from trees, and even animal carrion in the wild! In captivity, they love fermenting bananas!

The **POSTMAN** (*Heliconius melpomene*) comes from Central and South America. This species has long, brightly coloured forewings but their coloration is extremely variable. Each population has a different pattern of black, yellow, white and orange markings which serve as a warning that they are poisonous to predators. Caterpillars eat passionflower leaves and butterflies drink nectar, so require sugar water and cut soft fruit. Adult Postman Butterflies also eat pollen, which increases their life span (to three months or more). Add open flowers (e.g. Hibiscus or Lantana) to your enclosure to watch your butterflies collect pollen on the coils of their proboscis.

The **GREAT ORANGE TIP** (*Hebomoia glaucippe*) is a beautiful species of butterfly. The upper surfaces of its wings are white, with large orange and black markings towards their tips. The caterpillar of the Great Orange Tip is a snake mimic. If disturbed, it lifts its head and can inflate the front portion of its body to resemble a snake in an attack posture. It eats the leaves of garlic, mustard and Lady's Smock. Interestingly, Great Orange Tip caterpillars have been documented to be cannibalistic, should a pair or more meet. The butterflies drink nectar and require sugar water and cut soft fruit.

Caligo eurilochus

The **BLUE MORPHO** (*Morpho peleides*) is one of the most beautiful butterflies of the world. The upper surface of its wings are iridescent blue and the wingspan may be up to 20cm! Caterpillars of this South American species eat leaves of clover (*Trifolium* spp.) wisteria (*Wisteria* spp.), velvet bean (*Mucuna* spp.), and the peanut plant (*Arachis* spp.). Adults prefer fermenting fruit (especially mangos, kiwis, and lychees), but they also drink nectar (offer sugar water and large open flowers, such as Hibiscus).

OWL BUTTERFLIES (*Caligo* spp.) are a large (up to 20cm wingspan) and interesting group. They have intricate brown, white and black markings on the underside of their wings, with two striking eye-spots that resemble owl eyes. The 'eyes' create the illusion of a false head, and startle enemies when the butterflies fly. The caterpillars eat the leaves of some species of *Heliconia*, banana and sugar cane plants. The adults feed on dishes of rotting fruit (especially bananas).

The **SCARLET MORMON** (*Papilio rumanzovia*) originates from the Philippines. It is a large and striking species with black wings with bright reddish pink patches close to the wing bases and on the undersides of the wings. The caterpillars eat the leaves of citrus plants, while the adults drink nectar and should be provided with sugar water, cut soft fruit (especially oranges) and large, open flowers (such as Hibiscus).

The **GOLDEN BIRDWING** (*Troides aeacus*) is a member of the birdwing group which includes the world's largest butterflies. In this species, the wings are largely black, except parts of the hindwings, which have brilliant yellow and black patterns. The caterpillars of this species eat the leaves of many species of Dutchman's pipe (*Aristolochia* spp.) and a few species of *Thottea*. Adults drink nectar and should be provided with sugar water, cut soft fruit (especially oranges) and large, open flowers (such as Hibiscus).

The **PUSS MOTH** (*Cerura vinula*) is a wonderful species to rear. The caterpillars eat willow and poplar leaves and grow quickly. When disturbed, they rear themselves up and expose a ring of red display colour on their neck and red flails on their forked tails. They may also squirt formic acid on an attacker as well! The adult moths are white with delicate grey and brown patterns. Adult Puss Moths do not feed and have short lives. This is a great species for young entomologists to rear!

The **AMERICAN MOON MOTH**, also known as the Luna Moth (*Actias luna*) has elegant lime green wings with small eye-spots, and a wingspan of up to 12cm across. The light green caterpillars eat the leaves of walnut, hickory, persimmon and sweet gum trees. The adult moths do not feed, and only live for about one week. This is an easy but impressive species to rear and is recommended for beginners.

The **PRIVET HAWKMOTH** (*Sphinx ligustri*) is easy to keep and ideal for beginners. Its caterpillars feed mainly on privet, but also on ash, honeysuckle and lilac leaves. Privet Hawkmoths have beautiful purple and white diagonal stripes on their lime green bodies. Adult Privet Hawkmoths have variable brown, white, black and pink patterns on their wings and body. Most hawkmoths feed as adults, and the Privet will take sugar water, and likes open fresh flowers (particularly honeysuckle) from which it will drink.

The handsome **EMPEROR MOTH** (*Saturnia pavonia*) has a wingspan of up to 6cm, and has prominent eye-spots on its brown, white and black patterned wings. The caterpillars are striped with bands of black and orange spots, and eat the leaves of Meadowsweet, heather, hawthorn, bramble and birch. In their adult form, Emperor Moths do not feed and only live two or three weeks.

The **GARDEN TIGER MOTH** (*Arctia caja*) has beautifully patterned brown and white forewings, and orange, black and blue hindwings and body. Caterpillars are known as 'woolly bears' because of their long hairs (that should not be touched). The larvae eat dock leaves, dandelions, dead-nettle, nettle, pussy willow and cabbage. Adult Garden Tiger Moths drink nectar from flowers and should be given sugar water and open fresh flowers (particularly honeysuckle) from which they will drink. This species can hibernate over winter in curled, fallen leaves.

The caterpillars of the **ELEPHANT HAWKMOTH** (*Deilephila elpenor*) are large, plump and have 'elephant skin' patterns of brown, cream and black, and conspicuous eye-spots towards the head. The caterpillars are said to resemble an elephant's trunk, but when disturbed, they rise and display their eye-spots, more like a snake. The caterpillars eat Rosebay Willowherb (*Epilobium angustifolium*), bedstraws (*Galium* ssp.) and fuchsias. Adult Elephant Hawkmoths drink nectar from flowers and should be given sugar water and open fresh flowers (particularly honeysuckle), from which they will drink.

Although many species of moths may be used to produce silk, the **MULBERRY SILKMOTH** (*Bombyx mori*), known also as the Silk Worm, is the most commercially important. While neither the caterpillars nor the moths of this species are spectacular, the silk cocoons are really interesting and silk can easily be spun from them too! Caterpillars of this species eat mulberry leaves, which can be difficult to obtain. However, an artificial food substitute powder has recently been developed and makes rearing this species very simple. Several distinct races exist, many of which produce different coloured cocoons (white, yellow and even pinkish). Eggs must be refrigerated. For this species, leaves may be laid flat rather than arranged upright in water containers. The Mulberry Silkmoth is also unusual in that caterpillars generally do not wander from fresh food plant leaves. For these reasons, this species may be reared easily in trays rather than in regular net cages. Interestingly, the Mulberry Silkmoth no longer exists in the wild. It is believed to have originated in China and was domesticated over thousands of years.

The **ERI SILKMOTH** (*Samia cynthia ricini*) comes from Asia and is an easy to breed and impressive species with a wingspan up to 15cm. Its large wings have variable patterns of brown, white, pink and yellow. The yellow and black caterpillars grow very quickly (up to 7cm within one month). They eat the leaves of privet, as well as the foliage of castor beans, rhododendron, plum, apple, cherry trees and roses. The adult moths do not have mouths, and die after about 10 days. These beautiful moths are fascinating to see up close. If you wish to hold one, never grab it by the wings, but gently allow it to walk onto your hand so you can position it for viewing.

The **BULLSEYE MOTH** (*Automeris io*) ,also called the Io Moth, is interesting in that the two sexes of this species have different coloration: adult male Bullseye Moths have bright yellow wings, while the females' wings are reddish-brown. Both sexes have conspicuous black eye-spots on their hindwings, and smaller ones on their forewings. Caterpillars of this species should not be touched since they have branched, spines that sting. The larvae eat the leaves of apple, bramble, cherry, hazel, hawthorn, lime, oak, and willow. Bullseye Moths drink nectar from flowers and should be given sugar water and open fresh flowers (particularly honeysuckle), from which they will drink.

The **GIANT SILKMOTH** (*Hyalophora cecropia*) is North America's largest native moth. Specimens with wingspans up to 18cm across have been recorded. The caterpillars eat the leaves of maple trees, but also consume cherry and birch foliage. The wings of adults have beautiful patterns of brown, grey, black, white and brown. Adult moths of this species do not feed and live for only two weeks or so.

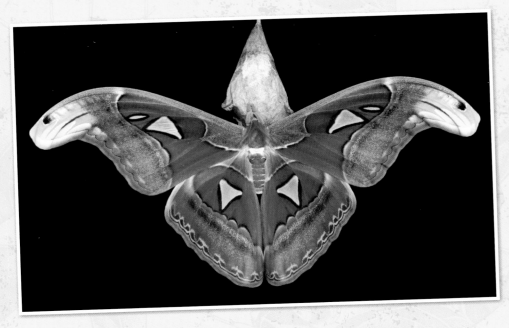

The **GIANT ATLAS MOTH** (*Attacus atlas*) is one of the world's largest and most spectacular moths. Caterpillars eat privet, as well as apple, ash, cherry, plum and willow. The larvae need to be kept warm (temperatures of 25–30°C), with high humidity, and preferably in a tank or plastic container rather than a netted cage. Adults require very large enclosures, for they have a wingspan up to 30cm (although populations of this species in parts of Asia may be considerably smaller but otherwise identical). Adult moths of this species do not feed and live for only a week or two.

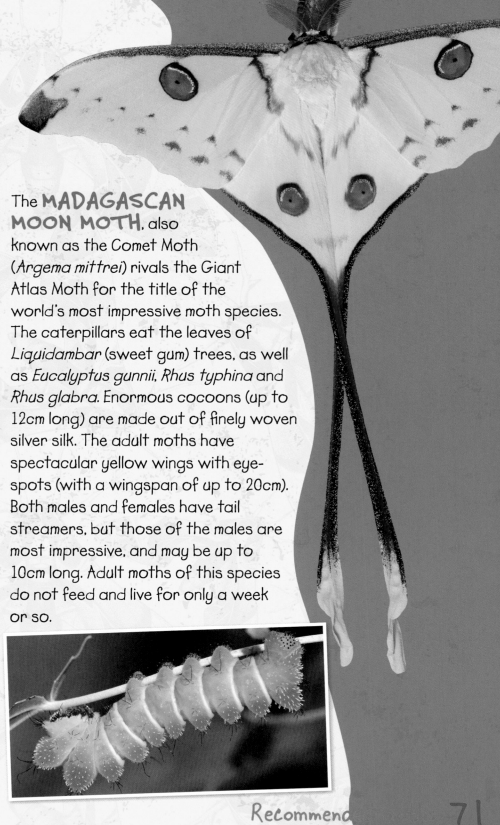

The **MADAGASCAN MOON MOTH**, also known as the Comet Moth (*Argema mittrei*) rivals the Giant Atlas Moth for the title of the world's most impressive moth species. The caterpillars eat the leaves of *Liquidambar* (sweet gum) trees, as well as *Eucalyptus gunnii*, *Rhus typhina* and *Rhus glabra*. Enormous cocoons (up to 12cm long) are made out of finely woven silver silk. The adult moths have spectacular yellow wings with eye-spots (with a wingspan of up to 20cm). Both males and females have tail streamers, but those of the males are most impressive, and may be up to 10cm long. Adult moths of this species do not feed and live for only a week or so.

HOW TO KEEP BUTTERFLIES & MOTHS

Many species of butterfly and moth are easy to keep, but the species that are available to you depend on where you live and the season. Your local supplier will be able to give advice. You will need a source of eggs, caterpillars or pupae depending upon the species, or where in the life cycle you wish to start. You must also be able to find a reliable supply of the food(s) that they eat. Your supplier will advise you on what works.

The following equipment is suggested:

1 An enclosure like a fine-meshed box or netted cage. For species requiring higher humidity, tall glass or plastic terrariums may be suitable, provided they are well ventilated. If you have a warm conservatory, the entire space may be used as a habitat!

2 Leafy stems of the correct food plants in a water container or a wet florist's foam block

3 A spray bottle/mister

4 An infrared heat source (if temperatures are too low).

Suitable enclosures

Eggs and caterpillars can be kept in relatively small containers about 20cm long, wide and high, although larger caterpillars and the winged adults will need a larger space. It is often easier to start in the enclosure they will live in as adults. This is important: many caterpillars will not eat fallen leaves, so there must be enough space to stand the stems of food plants upright.

Base of enclosure

Unless high humidity is required, paper can be used to line the base of the enclosure, making it easy to dispose of the droppings that fall to the floor. For tropical species, a few centimetres of damp soil at the base will help to maintain higher humidity levels.

Suitable net enclosures
for butterflies

Other requirements

It is not usually necessary to provide water in a bowl, as caterpillars usually acquire all the water they need from their diet. However, a very light misting with a spray bottle can sometimes be provided to make sure that the humidity is high enough.

A fully set up butterfly and moth enclosure

Feeding larvae

The caterpillars of each species of butterfly and moth eat the leaves of particular types of plants. If the incorrect food plant is given, caterpillars will starve and die. An important basic rule that you should consider before obtaining any eggs or caterpillars is: if you cannot supply the correct food, do not get the butterfly or moth.

Despite the fact that many species in captivity come from faraway places and usually eat plants you may never have heard of, many of them will eat some types of plants that can be sourced in your home country. You may need to collect branches of leaves, or grow entire plants to provide food for your caterpillars.

Food plants should always be fresh, and wilted or dead leaves should be removed. If you stand stems of food plants in a bottle or jar of water, ensure that the neck of the jar is blocked with cotton wool, tissue paper, foil or plastic wrap to prevent the caterpillars falling into the water and drowning. An alternative is to use florists' floral foam soaked with water.

Food should always be present, as caterpillars are voracious feeders and must be able to eat (and drink as they do so) whenever they wish. Some species can quickly die if left without food for even a short time. After pupation, adult butterflies and moths have completely different dietary requirements.

Feeding adult butterflies & moths

Some moths and butterflies emerge after metamorphosis without functional mouth parts and are incapable of feeding. Such species generally have short lives as adults, and naturally die after a few weeks. Other butterfly and moth species emerge as adults from their pupae with fully formed mouth parts and must feed in order to survive (sometimes several months) and reproduce.

Common foods for such adult butterflies and moths (mentioned over the following pages) are cut soft, sugar-rich fruit (such as oranges, bananas or nectarines) or artificial nectar 'sugar water' (a solution of 1 teaspoon sugar or honey to 10 teaspoons of water). Place sugar water in a small, shallow dish and put a small folded pad of kitchen paper at one end, soaked in the sugar water, to form a butterfly drinking station.

Ask your supplier about the exact needs of your pets, as different populations of certain species might have slightly different food preferences.

DID YOU KNOW?

Butterflies are able to taste, but rather than using their tongue-like proboscis, they taste with their FEET! By simply standing on their food, butterflies are able to use sensors similar to taste buds to decide whether a plant is worth feeding on!

Never handle hairy caterpillars with bare hands!

Holding your butterfly or moth

Butterflies and moths should not generally be handled as they are delicate and damaged limbs will not heal. Touching the wings causes the millions of tiny scales to be shed (the scales may cover your finger like dust). If adult butterflies and moths must be handled, it is best to do so using a very fine net made for use with these animals. If one escapes into the room, allow it to settle before trying to catch it, as snatching at it can easily result in injury.

Holding your caterpillar

Really tiny, baby caterpillars can be moved using a soft, dry paint brush. While many caterpillars are harmless, others have hairs and spines that can cause itchy or even painful reactions, never handle these caterpillars with bare hands! The hairs and spines are to discourage birds and other predators from eating the caterpillars (which otherwise would make a good meal). Most caterpillars have very delicate, squishy bodies, and can be severely harmed or even killed if dropped! If you do handle your caterpillar, do so extremely carefully and never grab it between pinched fingers, but rather, allow it to gently walk onto your hand, fingers or even better a held leaf.

The wrong way to handle butterflies and moths!

The correct way to handle butterflies and moths

Birdwing chrysalis

Looking after pupae

Caterpillars will generally shed their skin four to six times before they are ready to pupate. When ready, the caterpillars will often change behaviour, becoming restless and exploring their enclosure after a particularly heavy feed. Once a suitable site is chosen, either on the food plant, or the roof or floor of the enclosure, they will begin to make their pupa in the form of a chrysalis or cocoon. Some species will pupate by spinning silk amongst leaves and debris to make a cocoon, others do not have this extra protection with their chrysalis hanging from underneath leaves or branches. In a few species, the larvae burrow deeply into the soil and construct a subterranean chamber in which to pupate.

The pupae do not usually need to be moved, only maintained in stable conditions suitable for the species. For some species, very light and infrequent misting may be needed if conditions are dry. Discuss pupation needs of any butterfly and moth species with your supplier.

Breeding butterflies or moths

If you have adult male and female butterflies, keeping them together is usually enough to guarantee a successful mating. Eggs are laid on the caterpillars' food plants, which you'll need to place in the enclosure. Some species require plenty of space in which to perform courtship flights, whereas others require no space at all, but the species commonly available in the trade are often the easiest to breed. Always be sure to ask your supplier.

Hawkmoth chrysalis

Puss Moth cocoon

Once eggs have been laid, the adults will die. If they are in good condition, they can be beautifully mounted in display cases, a practice that is a hobby in its own right – in fact, many suppliers sell their dead adults by mail order just for mounting! The newly laid eggs should be left to develop alongside a fresh source of their correct food, in conditions ready for the emergence of the hungry baby caterpillars.

Never release captive bred butterflies and moths, even if they are native to the area in which you live. The strain of the particular species you are rearing may not be the same as the strain that occurs locally, and this can impact the wild population of your area. It is particularly important not to release non-natives species into the wild, as such individuals are not likely to survive for long, and could put native wildlife at risk.

Mating butterflies

A Monarch butterfly egg

The caterpillar forming

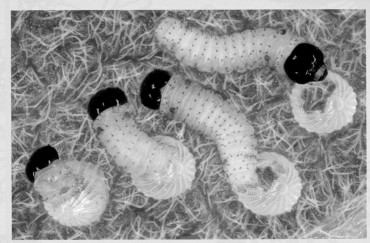

Caterpillars hatching and eating the egg case

Beetles

Beetles are some of the most familiar insects on Earth. There's a reason for that: the beetle group, the Coleoptera, is the largest animal group on the planet, with about 400,000 species! That means 40% of all insects are beetles, and there are eight times as many beetle species as there are amphibian, bird, fish, reptile and mammal species put together.

This tells us that beetles are one of the most successful and diverse animal groups in existence. They can adapt to almost all the terrestrial habitats found around the world, including freshwater. They are only absent from the extremely cold North and South Poles, and from the oceans. That said, some beetles live on beaches and in waters where freshwater and saltwater mix, so they are certainly doing their best to dominate the planet!

The name 'beetle' comes from the Old English bitel (little biting insect); however most beetles are placid and rarely bite. If they do, you are doing something wrong!

WHAT DOES A BEETLE LOOK LIKE?

Being such a big group, beetles come in all sorts of shapes and sizes, so there is a large amount of variation. Even so, the majority of beetles have a hard, protective exoskeleton, including protective wing cases (these are actually their forewings) that cover their hindwings (if present) which are used for flying.

As insects, their bodies are divided into the head, thorax and abdomen. They have a pair of antennae, mandibles (jaws) for eating, and their legs are divided into segments.

In many beetle species, the adult males and females can appear very different from one another. Males often have horns or claw-like jaws for grappling and battling!

The heads of beetle larvae are often protectively hardened, with well-formed chewing mouthparts. This allows some beetle larvae to burrow through soil or even rotting wood.

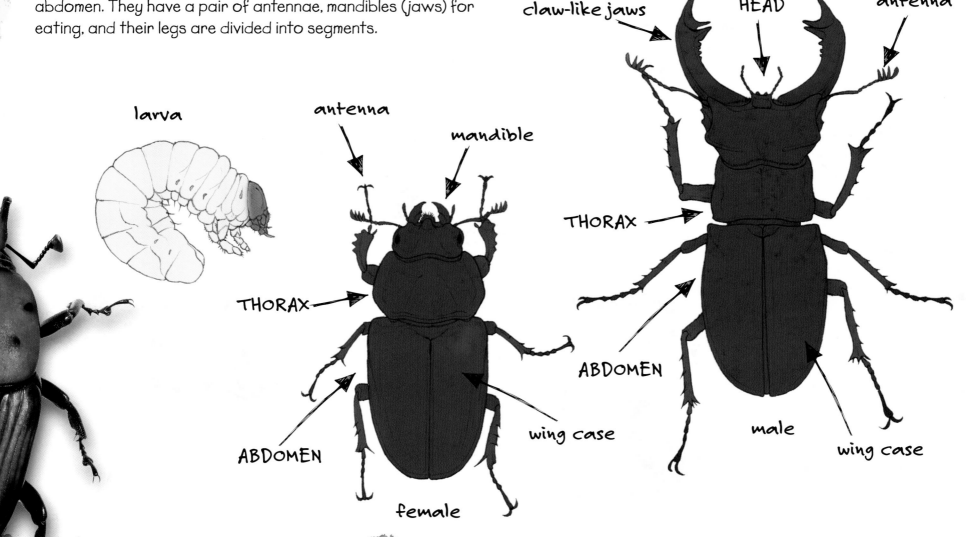

larva

antenna

mandible

THORAX

ABDOMEN

wing case

female

claw-like jaws

HEAD

antenna

THORAX

ABDOMEN

male

wing case

WEAPONRY

They may wear suits of armour, but most beetles bear no weapons, although a few, such as the male rhinoceros beetle with its large horns, normally used for battling rivals, look fearsome enough to possibly deter predators. Some predatory beetles, such as tiger beetles, do have powerful jaws for attacking prey.

HOW DO BEETLES FEED?

Beetles eat a broad range of foods. Many species are herbivores, consuming plants, fruits and vegetables in their larval and adult forms. Others are predatory, consuming mainly animals, particularly the eggs and larvae of other insects – and one type of beetle farms fungus, which it plants, harvests and consumes!

DEFENCE BEHAVIOUR

Although generally non-aggressive and placid, many beetle species have sharp mandibles and horns, and use these when threatened or cornered to defend themselves. Among these species are some of the largest insects on Earth (such as the Hercules Beetle, *Dynastes hercules*), whose horns are particularly powerful. A few species, such as male Frog Beetles (*Sagra buqueti*) have expanded rear legs that they may raise and snap closed in a pincer movement.

Other beetles defend themselves through camouflage – some may match the vegetation or decaying wood that they feed in. Many beetles simply roll over and play dead, while a few bury themselves to hide from predators when disturbed.

Some beetles do not try to camouflage themselves at all. Instead, they are brightly coloured, marked with very bright patches of contrasting colours like reds and yellows. These beetles are warning potential predators that they may be toxic and are not worth eating!

Releasing unpleasant chemicals is a very successful way to survive. While some beetles can create toxic tastes or smells, other harmless beetles mimic their colours to benefit from looking toxic too. Other otherwise harmless beetles concentrate toxic compounds from the food they eat in their tissues or specialised glands to use when necessary.

The Bombardier's Boiling Water Cannon!

The bombardier beetle opts for a different kind of chemical defence. It can accurately spray a caustic mix of chemicals and enzymes that spontaneously react as they mix, and reach boiling point, 100°C!

WHERE ARE BEETLES FOUND?

Beetles are found worldwide, in almost every habitat you can imagine on land and in fresh water. The only exceptions are Antarctica and the High Arctic, and marine (saltwater) habitats, which includes all the world's seas and oceans.

SCUBA DIVER BEETLES!

Believe it or not, some species of beetles have adapted to living in fresh water and can swim to depths of one metre or more in search of prey. The largest water beetles prey on other invertebrates, as well as tadpoles and even small fish! In addition to swimming and diving, some water beetles can also walk on dry land and fly as well.

Many water beetles carry an air bubble underneath their abdomen or beneath their wing cases. They use this bubble as an air supply, a bit like a scuba diver's tanks of air, and some species can stay underwater for many hours without needing to return to the surface for air!

FLYING BEETLES!

Most people know that beetles can fly, since the world's most recognisable beetle, the ladybird, is frequently seen doing just that. Of course, coming from such a large and diverse family, there are beetles that can't fly at all, but these are the minority. In fact, even the two largest beetles known, the Titan Beetle (*Titanus giganteus*) and the Hercules Beetle (*Dynastes hercules*), can fly, despite being the world's most massive insects!

LIFE CYCLE OF A BEETLE

Beetles go through a four-stage life cycle consisting of the egg, larval, pupa and adult stages. Most beetles lay eggs, which usually hatch after a few days or weeks. The soft, smooth eggs may be laid in soil, rotting wood, on plant stems and leaves, or even on the beetle's own back, depending on the species. When the larvae emerge they may consume their egg cases before they begin to feed voraciously.

Beetle larvae shed their skins a few times before forming pupae. As a larva consumes food it quickly grows, and each new skin will see it increase in size and sometimes develop additional features. Some beetle larvae proceed from egg to pupa to adult in a matter of days, but others may take months or years, particularly in areas with cold winter resting periods.

Once mature, a larva will pupate. Pupation involves a final shed that reveals an exoskeleton that rapidly hardens. The beetle pupa looks like a pale, mummified version of the adult, complete with legs and other appendages!

Finally, adult beetles emerge fully formed from their pupae. The adults, are sexually mature and capable of eating, unlike some other adult insects such as mayflies and many species of moth. Some adult beetles live for years, so it is important that they obtain much-needed energy and nutrition for survival and eventual breeding. Females rarely survive for long once they have laid eggs.

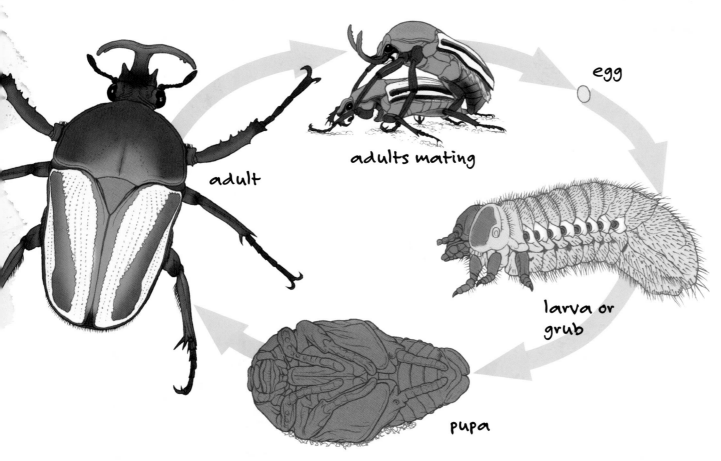

adult

adults mating

egg

larva or grub

pupa

Beetle larvae can vary tremendously between species, and while some eat living plants, others develop inside rotting logs consuming decaying wood. Some grubs grow beneath the ground consuming dead organic matter, and others are predatory and eat other insects or insects' eggs. Being such a large group of animals, virtually every type of diet has been documented amongst beetles!

RECOMMENDED BEETLES

With 400,000 beetle species known, the number of species in captivity is high, and varies depending upon where you are. Some of the most interesting and popular beetles in captivity are the colourful fruit beetles and armoured stag beetles.

Pachnoda sinuata

Pachnoda marginata

FRUIT CHAFERS, often known as Pachnoda beetles (*Pachnoda* spp.) are among the easiest species of beetles to rear and are highly recommended for beginners. Many species have short development periods (three to five months from egg to adult beetle) and then live as adults for up to five months.

There are many different *Pachnoda* species, each with different patterns of colour. *Pachnoda sinuata* is one of the most attractive, with bright yellow and jet black coloration, while *Pachnoda marginata* has more variable patches of mahogany brown set against lighter yellow.

The attractive **DERBY FLOWER BEETLE** (*Dicronorrhina derbyana*) comes from eastern Africa. This species is easily raised and very popular due to its shiny, metallic appearance, with striking bands of white between patches of green. The green patches are iridescent and appear orange or red from certain angles. The adults are 3.5–5cm long. The larvae feed on decaying oak and chestnut leaves, but adults should be fed soft fruit.

Dicronorrhina derbyana

Stephanorrhina guttata

SPOTTED FLOWER BEETLES

(*Stephanorrhina guttata*) have brightly iridescent backs tinged with green, orange, yellow and red, along with brilliant white spots. The adults can reach 2.5–3cm in length. It takes three to six months to raise these beetles from egg to adult. The adults survive for three to four months. The larvae feed on leaf litter, but the adults can be fed soft fruit, particularly banana.

Stephanorrhina guttata

The **AFRICAN GREEN FLOWER BEETLE**

(*Mecynorrhina polyphemus*) is rich green in colour with pale stripes down its thorax and variable spots or stripes on its wing cases. The males may be up to 8cm long, have horns (for battling one another) and are velvety, while the females reach 5.5cm long, lack horns and have shiny coloration. Adult beetles of this species may live up to five months.

Homoderus gladiator

Dynastes hercules

STAG BEETLES are a group of over 1,000 species. The males of most stag beetles have large and distinctive mandibles resembling deer antlers. These are used to fight with one another over females. Popular stag beetles in captivity include species of *Prosopocoilus savagei*, which are patterned with black, deep brown or tan, the chestnut brown *Homoderus gladiator* and the iridescent golden-green *Lamprima adolphinae* (see photo on page 81). The larvae of most stag beetles will feed on rotting woodchips and leaf humus, but the adults are more easily fed on banana and other soft fruits. The larvae may take as long as 15 months to mature, but some species develop more quickly. Adults may live for three months to a few years depending on the species.

Originating from Central America, the **HERCULES BEETLE** (*Dynastes hercules*) is a species of rhinoceros beetle and holds the title of 'longest beetle in the world'. In males, the body may be up to 8.5cm in length, in addition to impressive horns which may be 9cm long! The horns vary between specimens, but most breeders generally accept that properly fed and well looked after larvae give rise to the largest horns. Larvae can be raised in a soil consisting of shredded decomposing beech and oak leaves as well as rotting oak woodchips or chunks in a 80:20 ratio. Adults feed happily on banana. The larvae mature over the course of one to two years after hatching, and pupate for about two months before emerging as adults. Adult Hercules Beetles live three to six months.

HOW TO KEEP A BEETLE

Beetles make exciting and interesting pets, not least awaiting the metamorphosis of grubs into spectacular adults! To keep a beetle, you'll need the following pieces of equipment:

1 **A suitable enclosure. Larger beetles require more space, and if breeding, the soil depth is important for some species – up to 40cm deep for some stag beetles! Your supplier will advise you on a suitable size, but 40cm long, 30cm wide and 30cm deep is suitable for breeding many smaller beetles**

2 **A suitable soil based on humus or peat-free compost. If raising larvae, it might consist of shredded beech and oak leaves with leaf mould and chunks of rotten wood**

3 **For adults, soft fruits are popular, banana being the best general food item for many types of beetle**

4 **A heat source (if your home is too cold), ideally in the form of a heat lamp – temperatures of 18–24°C are suitable for a broad range of species, but tropical species will require 23–28°C.**

Suitable enclosures

If you are simply keeping adults, a glass or clear plastic tank with a tight-fitting lid and good ventilation is suitable for most beetles. A tank of about 30 × 20 × 30cm (length × width × height) can house a few pairs of adults.

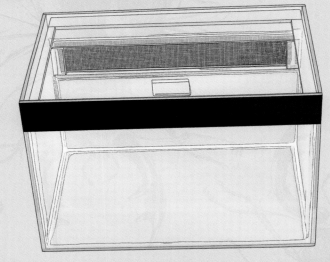

A suitable enclosure for keeping beetles

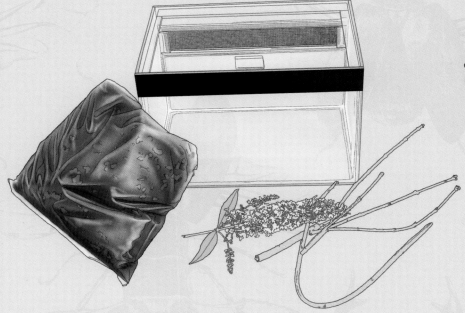

Items required for setting up a beetle enclosure

Soil for enclosure

A base (substrate) of damp soil 10cm deep is ideal, but when breeding this may need to be 30–40cm deep for large beetles. As a general rule, soil consisting of peat free compost or coco-fibre (40%) mixed with deciduous leaf litter (60%) from healthy local woodlands is ideal. Avoid litter and humus that has been treated with any kinds of chemicals. For specific beetle species, the type of leaves used may be important. For example, oak and beech are good for stag beetles.

The mixed substrate should be moist, rather than sopping wet, and should more or less form a ball when cupped tightly between two hands – if not, the leaves may need to be broken down further by shredding. If the soil releases water when squeezed tightly, it is too wet.

Water

It is not necessary to provide water, as beetles and their larvae acquire sufficient amounts from their food. However, to avoid their soil drying out through evaporation, carefully add clean, chlorine-free water from time to time. Tap water is fine if it is first boiled and then left to cool for several hours.

If in doubt, it is better to add too little water than too much, as adding more water is easily done – removing the excess is not! For this reason, larger enclosures can be easier to manage, as the larger soil volume is more stable in terms of moisture.

Other requirements

Once the soil is in place, arrange some branches and small rocks to landscape the tank. These will help adult beetles to turn themselves over when they fall onto their backs (which they will do!), and also provide shelters where they will feel safe.

For tropical beetles, a thermostatically controlled heat source may be required if your home is too cool. A heat lamp can be useful, as it warms the top layer of the tank but not the bottom, allowing the beetles a choice of warmer or cooler places. However, for breeding beetles, a heat pad set to 18–20°C will help warm up soil that may be too cool. Even tropical soils are cool at depth, so there is no need to exceed those temperatures, but colder temperatures may cause problems.

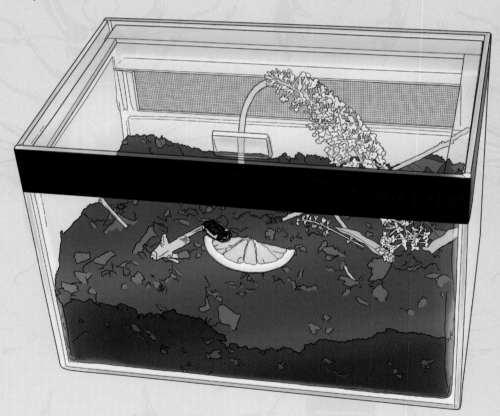

A fully set up beetle enclosure

Some specialist suppliers provide beetle food in the form of specially formulated jellies. These can be used to supplement or replace the usual diet of fruits, since they often contain beneficial nutrients that can be in short supply.

Feeding your beetle

Beetle larvae consume mainly decaying leaves and wood, and this can be supplemented with wheatgerm from a health food shop. The quantities should be one part wheatgerm to nine parts decaying leaves and wood. Your supplier will advise you about the specific needs of the species you choose to keep. Failing that, there are numerous online resources that can advise you.

Adult beetles are easier to look after, as most in captivity will happily consume soft, sugary fruit, banana being a particular favourite, though nectarines, peaches and soft apples are all readily consumed. Fruit should be replaced after a day or two to prevent spoilage in the tank, as fungi may start to grow in your enclosure, and some of these may put your beetles at risk.

Holding your beetle

Most beetles are relatively docile and will tolerate being held, but some individuals may show distress when picked up. It is best to coax beetles onto your fingers by gently prodding them from behind. For those with mandibles that are prone to bite, it can be safest to gently pick them up by grasping either side of their thorax and placing them onto your hand.

Breeding beetles

Adult beetles often find their mates by following scents. This is because females may produce attractive scents to announce that they are ready for sexual activity. Others, like fireflies (which are beetles, not flies!), rely on bioluminescence (creating light) to communicate with their mates.

Males may battle for the attention of females. Rhinoceros beetles will lock horns and 'rut' like male deer do. The victorious male will then court the female by vibrating his body against objects, making noises by rubbing his legs or wings together, or caressing her with his antennae. When the time is right, he will mount the female and fertilise her eggs.

Male and female beetle pairs will mate soon after they have emerged and fed. It may be sensible to keep them apart initially if you wish to observe the females for any length of time as once they breed, she will lay her eggs and die.

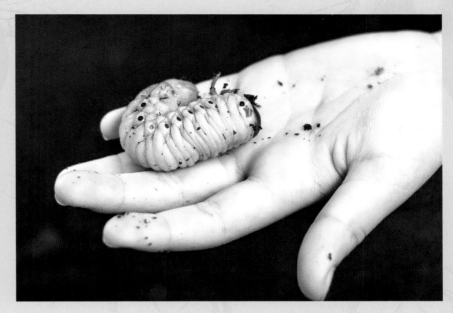

After mating, the female will burrow down into the soil to lay her eggs. The number of eggs can vary from one to a few hundred, so be sure to find out what is usual for your species. The female will not usually re-emerge, so you will need to retrieve her body when changing the soil.

Once the eggs hatch, the small, white larvae will immediately start to feed on organic matter within the soil. These grubs can be left in the soil, but can be easier to manage if housed in separate containers. To retrieve them, carefully tip out the soil and simply sift through it to collect the eggs and grubs, which are often at different stages of development. Place those at similar stages of development in the same containers. Every few weeks, remove some of the soil and replace it with fresh material. After several months of feeding, the larvae will have grown significantly and will eventually pupate. This two to three month process should take place in a full-sized tank and should not be interrupted – the adult will develop and emerge without your help.

When preparing deep soil for breeding beetles, compact the soil with your fingertips. The lowest 10cm should be pressed down hard, to provide a base on which eggs can be laid, the rest of the soil should be gently compacted to try to ensure that there are no large gaps (air pockets) in the soil. The larvae of many beetles will also dig down into the compacted layer to pupate.

The soil is food for larvae, so it is important that the material used is free of insecticides. Many livestock suppliers that offer a large selection of beetle species also sell specialist beetle medium which serves as perfect substrate for your beetle enclosure!

Giant millipedes

Millipedes are group of segmented animals, usually with elongated bodies. The majority of the segments have two pairs of jointed legs. The name 'millipede' means 'thousand footed', but most millipedes have between 47 and 197 pairs of legs. The record for the greatest number of feet belongs to a Californian millipede with 375 pairs of legs – that's 750 legs in total, about twice as many as most other millipedes! Millipedes first appeared between 419–443 million years ago, making them one of the most ancient of all animal groups.

Giant millipedes include typical-looking species with long, cylindrical bodies, but also plated millipedes, which produce protruding plates of exoskeleton that looks like armour, and finally pill millipedes (or giant pill bugs), which look like oversized woodlice – they are often capable of rolling up into almost perfect defensive ball!

WHAT DO THEY LOOK LIKE?

Millipedes can be long and slender or short and broad. The giant millipedes mainly have a rounded head with a pair of relatively short, segmented antennae, as well as a large pair of mandibles (jaws) for eating. Their bodies are usually more or less cylindrical, and most body segments bear two pairs of legs that stick out on either side of the body. The segments are covered with plates of rigid exoskeleton (tergites). The first three segments after the head and neck (collum) often have just one pair of legs. Millipedes breathe through tiny holes (spiracles) positioned in pairs on the underside of each segment and connected to an internal network of tiny airways, like insects. Millipede 'eyes' are simply patches of light-sensitive organs called ocelli, so their vision is poor, and many species are actually blind!

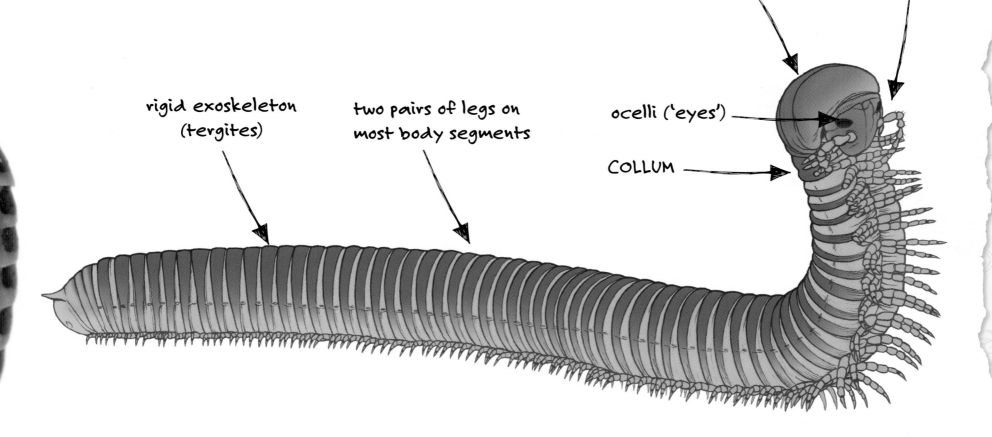

HEAD

antenna

ocelli ('eyes')

COLLUM

rigid exoskeleton
(tergites)

two pairs of legs on
most body segments

WEAPONRY

Millipedes do not have any weaponry. Instead, they rely on defensive structures, like their hard exoskeleton, as well as certain behaviours. Their exoskeleton is divided into sets of plates attached to each segment, usually with one arching plate covering the top, one for the underside and two smaller plates on each side to protect their flanks.

HOW DO GIANT MILLIPEDES FEED?

Giant millipedes are herbivores and only consume plants, usually consisting of dead and decaying materials. Most species will also consume fresh plant material, making it easier to cater for their needs in captivity. Millipedes are often nocturnal, foraging at night for food in leaf litter and on tree trunks. This nocturnal habit offers protection in two ways: firstly, they are less easily spotted by predators in the dark, allowing them to roam safely, and secondly, they can become easily dehydrated in sunlight, which they avoid by feeding at night!

DEFENCE BEHAVIOUR

When they identify a threat, millipedes will curl up into a tight spiral. This puts their tough exoskeleton on the outside, while protecting their soft and vulnerable undersides.

POISON SPRAY

Many millipedes can also spray a strong-smelling liquid that drives away predators. This can contain hydrocyanic acid (HCN) which is a toxic irritant. However, giant millipedes are generally docile and rarely produce significant amounts when gently handled. Even so, after handling them it is always wise to wash your hands before you touch your eyes or mouth, as small amounts of this fluid may end up on your skin. If it does, you'll often be able to smell it as it has a rather peculiar odour.

Millipedes use colour in various ways. Many species are brown or black – good camouflage amongst the leaf litter in which they live. Other species take a completely different approach and have brightly coloured segments (so appear stripy) or brightly coloured feet. In these cases, the bright colours (often red, yellow, orange and blue) warn potential predators that the millipede has a foul taste or may even be toxic if eaten!

WHERE ARE GIANT MILLIPEDES FOUND?

While millipedes occur worldwide, giant ones are known only from the tropical rainforests of Southeast Asia, tropical and subtropical Africa, and from tropical parts of the Americas.

How long is the longest millipede? The Giant African Millipede, *Archispirostreptus gigas*, from East Africa, sets the record for millipedes, being the longest and heaviest, with individuals up to 38.5cm recorded.

Some millipedes have extremely narrow bodies. The Siphonophorid millipedes grow up to 8cm long, but often have bodies just 1–3mm wide and so resemble a strand of spaghetti!

PREHISTORIC

The ancestors of modern millipedes were among the very first animals to adapt to live permanently on land. The first fossil millipedes date back to around 420–450 million years ago.

Around 315–299 million years ago, during the late Carboniferous Period, higher levels of oxygen in the Earth's atmosphere and a lack of large predators allowed gigantic millipedes to evolve and roam the land! Fossils of 2.3m long *Arthropleura* have been discovered in Scotland and North America! This truly giant millipede had 30 jointed body segments. Its fossilised tracks are up to 50cm wide and suggest that this plant eater moved really quickly along the prehistoric forest floor!

LIFE CYCLE OF A GIANT MILLIPEDE

Giant millipedes hatch from eggs laid in moist ground material such as soil or leaf mould. The young hatch after a number of weeks and emerge with quite short bodies. In addition to the head and neck, the young have just three segments with one pair of legs each, plus two to four legless segments depending upon the species, and the anal segment, from where they get rid of bodily waste.

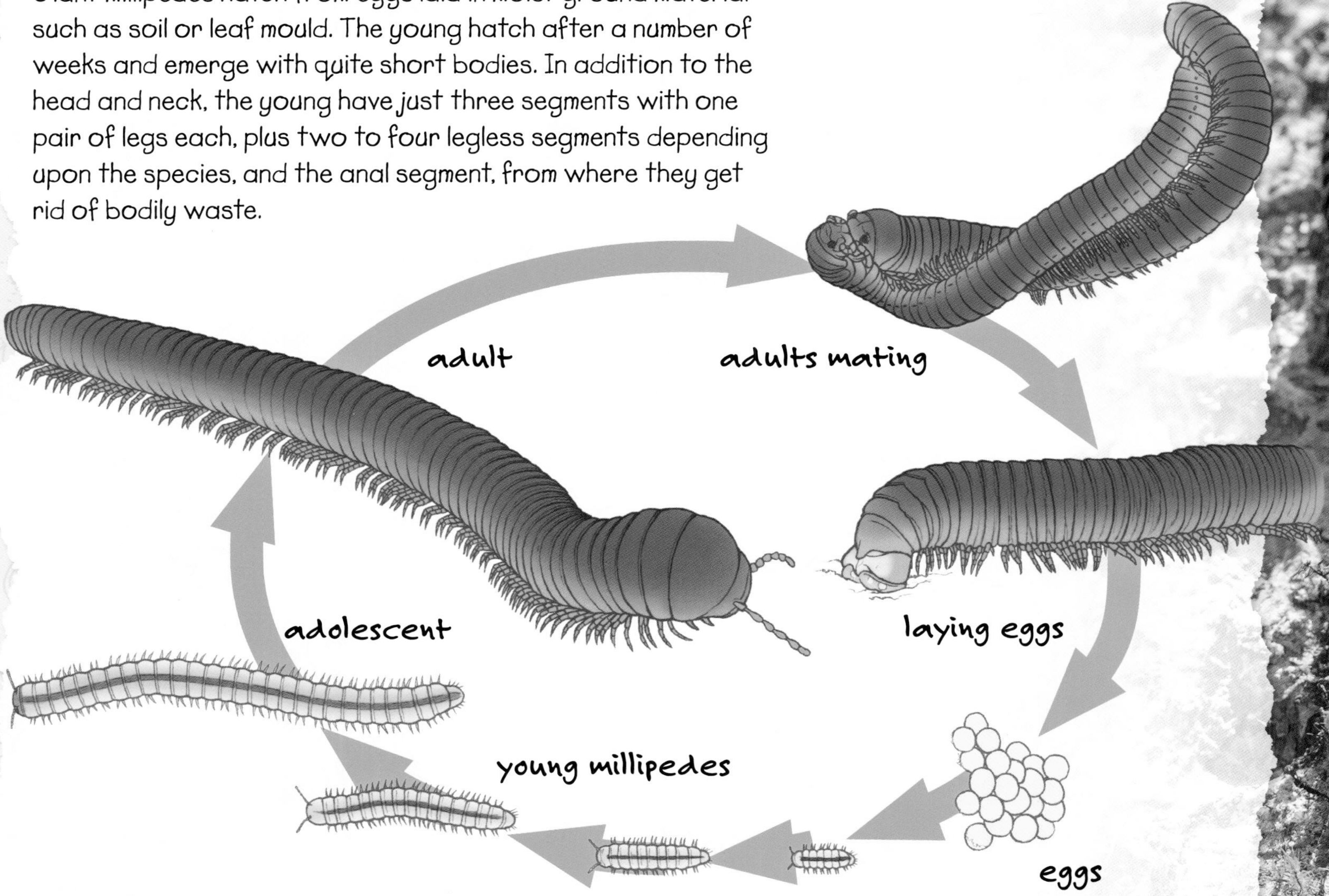

adult

adults mating

adolescent

laying eggs

young millipedes

eggs

As the young millipedes feed and grow, they periodically shed their skins, giving rise to additional segments and legs each time. Millipedes will shed their skin many times before reaching sexual maturity (between 4 and 20 times depending upon the species). After that they only shed periodically as they increase more slowly in size.

RECOMMENDED GIANT MILLIPEDES

Though there are about 12,000 species of millipede, there are only tens of species that are regarded as giant. They come in a diverse range of forms and colours, and many of them are kept in captivity. The species available to you will depend on where you live, as some countries forbid foreign imports.

Dozens of other giant millipede species are reared in captivity, and come in a variety of sizes and colours. The **BUMBLEBEE MILLIPEDES** (*Anadenobolus monilicornis*) has beautiful yellow bands and grows up to 10cm long. The **RUSTY MILLIPEDE** (*Trigoniulus corallinus*) is a reddish-brown, sometimes with darker bands, and can grow to a length of 16cm.

The **GIANT AFRICAN MILLIPEDE** (*Archispirostreptus gigas*) is the most widely reared giant millipede in captivity. It may grow up to 38.5cm in length, and healthy individuals may live up to seven years if properly cared for. Its body segments are dark brown, with lighter coloured legs.

Recommended plated millipedes

Several species of giant millipedes are known as **RAINBOW MILLIPEDES** for they have multicoloured bands of brown, black, grey, blue, red and orange. The most widely reared are *Tonkinbolus caudulanus* and *T. dolfusi*, which grow up to 10cm.

Several millipede species are also known as **RED-LEGGED MILLIPEDES** (such as *Ephibolus pulchripes*) for their pinkish or even bright red legs. Most species in captivity grow to between 10 and 15cm in length.

The protruding plates of exoskeleton in these millipedes makes them appear very robust – some people call them armoured or tractor millipedes! Though most species are black, brown or grey, some are bright blue, red or even purple! Some species in this group look very much like centipedes, but can be identified by the presence of two pairs of legs on the majority of their segments.

Plated millipedes are not very widespread in captivity. Among those most frequently reared are *Rhododesmus mastophorus* and various species of *Polydesmus* and *Orthomorpha*. These species grow up to about 4cm. Their care requirements are the same as for giant millipedes.

Giant pill millipedes

Giant pill millipedes are present through Southeast Asia, South Asia, Madagascar, southern Africa, Australia and New Zealand. They are so-called because they roll up into balls when threatened. They vary significantly in size; some as large as a cherry, and others as big as a golf ball! Pill millipedes are not commonly kept in captivity and are very difficult to rear (so not recommended for beginners). Among those most widely seen in captivity are: *Rhopalomeris carnifex* (a very colourful species with white, black, yellow and red markings) and *Arthrosphaera brandtii* (which has beautiful chocolate brown coloration).

MILLIPEDES AND CENTIPEDES: SIMILAR BUT DIFFERENT!

Although millipedes look similar to centipedes, their habits and dispositions are quite different. Millipedes are relatively slow-moving, mainly harmless detritivores that mostly consume dead or dying plant matter and fungi. Centipedes, on the other hand, are generally fast-moving, carnivorous predators – they have one pair of jointed legs per body segment; these are adapted to running and make their movements quite alarming! Centipedes are mostly venomous, and bear a pair of large, modified venomous claws close to the mouth that act as fangs. The two groups last shared a common ancestor about 450 million years ago, before modern millipedes even came into existence, so they are now quite distantly related!!

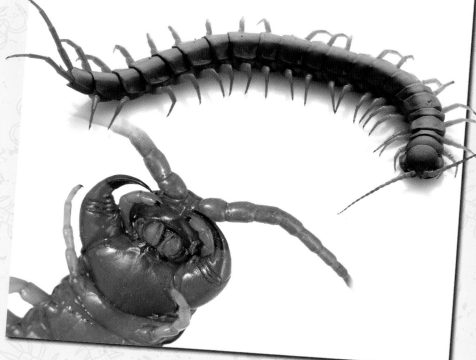

HOW TO KEEP GIANT MILLIPEDES

Most giant millipedes are easy to care for and make fascinating pets. The following guidelines apply to most types, but always check with your supplier to ensure that you understand the needs of individual species. To keep giant millipedes, you need the following pieces of equipment:

1 An enclosure such as a small aquarium

2 Soil at the bottom of the tank

3 A spray bottle/mister

4 A low-lying dish for food

5 A thermostatically controlled heat source such as a heat pad (if room temperatures are too low.

Suitable enclosures

Giant millipedes do well in a range of enclosures, including small fish tanks, terrariums or large, ventilated plastic jars. To ensure adequate space, enclosures should be at least twice as long as the millipede, and as wide as the millipede is long. Mesh boxes are not suitable for these animals as they require moderate to high humidity, depending on the species. Even so, a good enclosure will have good ventilation, as stagnant air can lead to ill health. One way to avoid stagnant air is to use an enclosure with a mesh top.

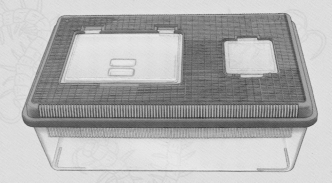

A suitable enclosure for keeping giant millipedes

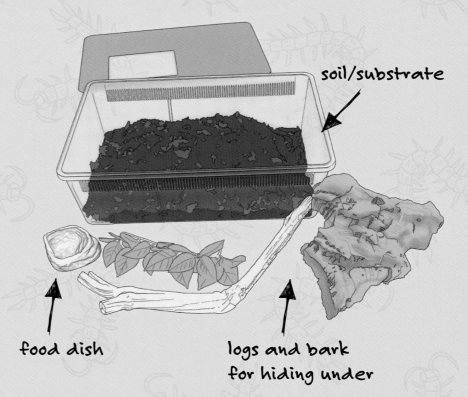

soil/substrate

food dish

logs and bark for hiding under

Setting up a giant millipede enclosure

Soil for enclosure

By lining the bottom of the enclosure with soil, you can maintain reasonably high humidity by simply adding clean water to the base of the tank – the soil should be damp, but not wet. The soil layer should be 5–10cm deep so that the millipede can burrow. An ideal soil will consist of peat-free compost, sand and finely chipped bark, or a similar combination. Leaf litter can be used, but this should be heat sterilised beforehand to avoid introducing wild insects or pests that may harm your millipede.

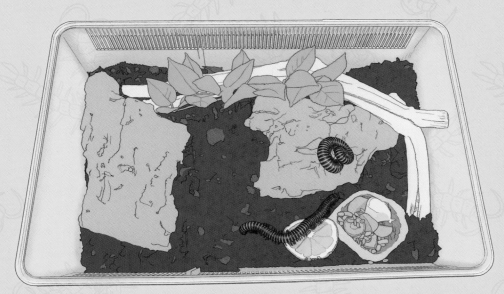

A fully set up giant millipede enclosure

Other requirements

Enclosures should be maintained at 24–28°C for most species of giant millipede. To provide such temperatures, it may be necessary for you to install a heat pad (available from reptile stores and pet shops). Note: if you install a heat pad, it should be installed vertically (on one of the sides of the tank), not horizontally, underneath the tank. The reason for this is that millipedes have an instinct to dig downward when they are too hot. If you place the heat pad underneath the tank, and conditions are too warm, your millipede will dig down in the substrate in its enclosure and get closer to the heat pad and likely die from overheating.

Do not place tanks near sunlit windows or near bright light sources as millipedes prefer shady undergrowth in nature. Millipedes usually receive ample moisture from their diets and will not need to drink often, but a small, shallow dish of water placed in the enclosure will ensure that they do not go thirsty.

Feeding your giant millipede

Although giant millipedes usually consume dead or dying vegetable matter in the wild, they will happily eat living material in captivity. Ideal food items include potato and apple peels, lettuce, sliced cucumber, tomatoes, peaches and banana. Sweeter items are best provided in smaller quantities as treats.

It is fine to leave food in the enclosure for one or two days, as some species prefer to eat food that is softer and discoloured. This usually starts to happen as the food starts to decay. However, food should be periodically replaced and the tank kept otherwise clean to prevent the development of disease. Calcium supplements should be used to occasionally dust the food – you can do this as directed by your supplier.

MILLIPEDES CAN SING!

When initiating mating, the males of three groups of millipedes will 'stridulate', producing sound by rubbing parts of their exoskeleton together. The vibration is thought to signal their intentions to the females.

Holding your giant millipede

Giant millipedes prefer not to be handled regularly, but they can be safely handled on a weekly basis if necessary. This can be done ideally by coaxing them onto a hand laid in front of them. They can then crawl from one hand to the other. Never try to grab them by the body, as this can cause stress.

Although millipedes are relatively slow moving, make sure that you supervise younger children who handle them, in case they drop them. Once the millipede has been placed back into its enclosure, ensure that you thoroughly wash your hands with soap to ensure that its irritant secretions do not come into contact with your eyes or mouth.

Breeding giant millipedes

It is hard to tell male and female millipedes apart, but generally the males have a specialised set of legs used for breeding tucked away in their seventh segment. This appears as a gap if the animal is studied from the side.

If kept together and conditions are good, males and females will eventually breed: the pair will clasp each other and the male will pass sperm to the female, which she is able to store for a long period. The female lays her eggs beneath the soil and these will hatch into young in a matter of weeks. The young need no special care and can be safely kept alongside their parents without risk of cannibalism.

Triops

Also known as tadpole shrimps, triops are a group of small crustaceans (the family of crabs, shrimps, woodlice and barnacles) whose ancestors first appeared about 300 million years ago. Although they are often called living fossils, they are constantly adapting in response to their environment. There are ten recognised species of triops and at least four of them are regularly kept as pets.

The name *Triops* comes from Greek and means 'three eyes'. It was given to these animals in 1803 because of the three eyes that can easily be seen towards the front of their shield-like carapace.

WHAT DO THEY LOOK LIKE?

The body of triops consists of the head, thorax and abdomen. The protective shell-like carapace is an extension of one of the head segments. The head has a pair of compound eyes which sit at the top of the carapace either side of the third eye (the naupliar eye). This third eye can detect light from above, through the carapace, and also below the animal. Beneath the eyes is a set of mandibles (jaws) that break up food into smaller pieces for eating.

The thorax consists of numerous segments. The front 11 segments have paired, leg-like appendages called thoracopods – these are mainly used to move, although the front pair are divided and extremely elongated into what look like antennae. These also act like antennae, as they are sensory organs used to explore the environment.

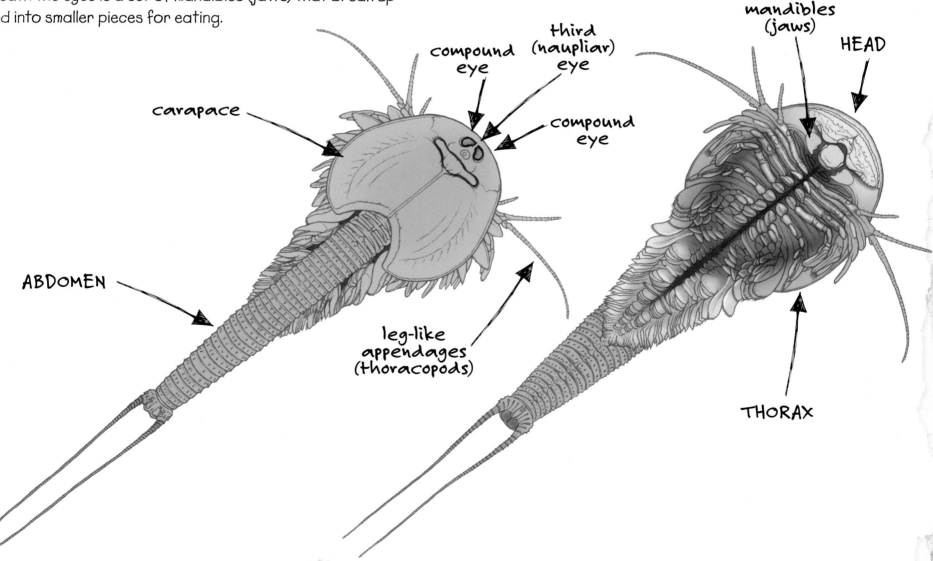

compound eye

third (naupliar) eye

compound eye

mandibles (jaws)

HEAD

carapace

ABDOMEN

leg-like appendages (thoracopods)

THORAX

HOW DO TRIOPS FEED?

Triops are omnivores, which means that they are able to eat a variety of animal or plant material, provided it is small enough. They will graze on algae and small, floating debris, but can also feed on insect larvae, tadpoles, small aquatic worms and the hatchlings of fish.

Triops use the modified legs beneath their bodies to sweep food up a central groove that runs from the rear underside of the thorax to the mouth. They then use their mandibles to break the food up into more managable pieces before they eat it.

DEFENCE BEHAVIOUR

Triops are relatively simply organisms that mainly rely on their carapace for protection. They are great survivors and in shallow, temporary pools they are typically the top predators, consuming smaller animals like *Daphnia* (water fleas) and mosquito larvae. However, in larger ponds, they are known to be eaten by frogs and newts, and sometimes even by birds.

WHERE ARE TRIOPS FOUND?

Triops can be found on every continent except Antarctica, which is too frozen for them. This is because they first appeared on the ancient supercontinent Pangaea. So they were able to spread across Pangaea before it broke up into the present-day continents and have survived ever since!

PREHISTORIC PETS

Triops are sometimes called 'living fossils' because fossilised remains that are virtually identical to modern day triops species have been found in 180 million year old rocks of the Jurassic Period. The very earliest fossils that are recognisable as triops date back to the Carboniferous age, approximately 300 million years ago! These are truly ancient creatures that have changed very little over time!

Did you know?

Triops do not need to mate in order to reproduce. Young can hatch from unfertilised eggs so that even if a single triops lives alone in a particular pool, the population can survive to subsequent years. In many triops species, males are very rare, and in some populations, the majority of (or possibly even all) breeding takes place without mating! This method of reproduction could be one reason why triops have changed very little over millions of years.

Larger triops will also eat their younger siblings. As only one triops is required to lay fertile eggs, eating your family members can provide enough energy to produce the next generation all by yourself!

LIFE CYCLE OF A TRIOPS

Triops are found in seasonally wet habitats that dry out for part of the year, and yet can survive from one season to the next. Their extraordinary eggs have a thick shell that has evolved to withstand extreme heat (up to 98°C) and cold, drought and even radiation. In fact, once the eggs have been laid, they will not hatch until they have dried out completely first, and they can survive in a state of suspended animation for several decades until good conditions return.

Once the dry period ends and their habitat becomes wet again, the eggs hatch. The tiny larvae that emerge have just one eye and three pairs of legs. They start to feed almost immediately and grow rapidly. As they increase in size, they shed their skins, each time gaining segments and additional structures. They will usually reach maturity in seven to ten days, after which they will quickly start to lay eggs in case their habitat starts to dry out.

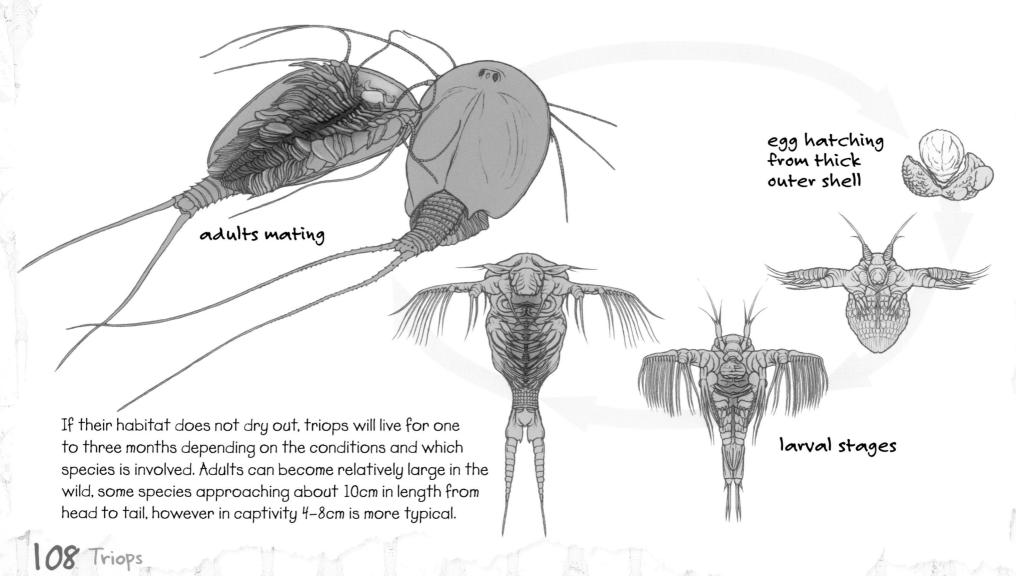

adults mating

egg hatching from thick outer shell

larval stages

If their habitat does not dry out, triops will live for one to three months depending on the conditions and which species is involved. Adults can become relatively large in the wild, some species approaching about 10cm in length from head to tail, however in captivity 4–8cm is more typical.

Suitable enclosures

Small fish tanks or deep dishes made of glass or plastic are ideal for raising triops. Glass is easier to keep clean and will not discolour over time, while plastic is lighter and cheaper.

A slightly larger container may seem unnecessary, but the conditions inside it will be more stable, which is good for the health of your triops. This is because larger volumes of water do not experience temperature fluctuations as quickly as smaller volumes of water do. It is also harder to foul a larger volume of water, which can happen quickly in small tanks and jars if the animals are overfed. Remember, however, that triops naturally occur in shallow water, and while a large surface area is good for them, deep water may not contain the ideal concentrations of dissolved oxygen that they need.

Setting up a triops tank

HOW TO KEEP TRIOPS

Triops have basic needs and are quite easy to look after, provided you keep their tanks clean. To keep them you will need:

1 A small tank 15cm long and wide, with a depth of 6–10cm. However, larger tanks require less frequent cleaning and offer more stable conditions

2 Triops eggs

3 Bottled distilled water

4 A dependable food source.

A fully set up triops tank

Other requirements

Triops require clean water that is free of chemicals and mineral salts. As such, tap water is not usually suitable, particularly in urban areas. The best options are bottled distilled water and spring water, avoiding water from mineral springs as these can be high in dissolved solids. Triops should be kept in warm, stable conditions from about 23–28°C, so room temperature conditions are usually adequate. For best results, they should be illuminated during the day with a water-safe aquarium lamp, which mimics natural sunlight.

A layer of aquarium sand or fine pebbles in the bottom of the container will provide the triops with a place to lay their eggs. The layer will also delay the rate at which the water becomes foul. It is important not to use beach or builder's sand as these will contain harmful mineral salts.

Hatching triops

Your triops will normally arrive in the form of a packet of eggs, often with a small tank and some food. You should set up the tank for your triops a few days before you intend to hatch the eggs so that the conditions in the tank settle. If adding a substrate like sand, place 1cm of the substrate in the bottom of the tank, then carefully fill the tank with bottled water and leave it to settle (placing a shallow saucer on the sand and pouring the water gently into that will stop the sand from being stirred up too much). Once the tank is ready, simply add the eggs and wait. Hatching usually occurs within 24–48 hours, the young appearing as very tiny, almost-transparent moving dots!

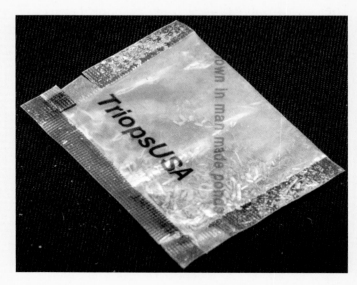

Feeding your triops

Triops grow rapidly and will begin to feed soon after they hatch. On the third day after the eggs are added to the water, you can start feeding them. Either use the food provided with the eggs, or use crushed flakes of fish food sold for tropical fish, feeding them a few crushed flakes once per day for the first two to three days. Remove any uneaten food after a few hours. Thereafter, you should feed them two to three times per day, allowing them to eat until they stop feeding. It is important to remove the extra food using a fine net so that the water does not become cloudy and start to smell. After about one week the triops will be about 5mm long. They will grow rapidly from this point on and should be fed sufficient amounts to stop them from eating each other.

Since triops eat many different kinds of foods, you can also provide them with small pieces of carrot, bloodworms or even ornamental marimo algae balls sold online via eBay and at aquarium shops. These are beneficial in that they are less likely to foul the water, but they may not be as easy to come by.

If the water starts to become cloudy, or if it develops an unpleasant smell, fill a container with fresh bottled water and place it next to your triops tank for a few hours so that it reaches the same temperature. Then, using a small cup or bowl, remove about a third of the fouled water from your triops tank and pour it down the drain, being careful to make sure you don't remove any triops! Replace the water you poured away with fresh water from the container. After a few hours, repeat the process. It is important not to replace all the water at once as the shock of changing the water can result in death of your triops.

Breeding triops

Once the triops are about two to three weeks old, they will achieve sexual maturity and start to lay eggs in the substrate. Once they have laid a few times, they will simply die and should be removed from the tank. When all the triops are dead, remove most of the water and then allow the substrate to dry out completely for a few weeks. Then, to start the hatching of the eggs in the sand, simply refill the tank with fresh, clean water and wait for the young to emerge!

Giant land snails

Snails are instantly recognisable around the world as the spiral-shelled members of the gastropod family, a group that they share with slugs, their closest relatives. While most snails are relatively small, typically 2–5cm in diameter, there are some very large species. The largest of these are the African giant land snails, of which there are three main groups containing dozens of species. However, only two, *Lissachatina fulica* and *Achatina achatina*, are frequently kept as pets – both are known by the common name Giant African Snail. These snails make good pets, but are banned in some countries, so it is important to make sure that they are legal where you live. The reason they are sometimes banned is that irresponsible owners have released them into the wild in some places, where they have become pest species that destroy crops and compete with native animals. It is legal to keep them in the UK and some other European countries, but it is illegal to introduce them into the wild and their eggs must be destroyed if they are not being kept for hatching more pets.

WHAT DO THEY LOOK LIKE?

The bodies of giant land snails are typical of other land snails, only much larger, their shells reaching over 20cm in length and 10cm in diameter! Like most land snails, their shells are conical, into which they can retract. They move on a muscular foot which is lubricated by a special mucus, have eyes on a pair of stalked, retractable tentacles, and breathe through a simple, specialised lung evolved from gills (some types of land snail still have gills). Snails feed by scraping at their food with a ribbon-like structure in their mouths called a radula.

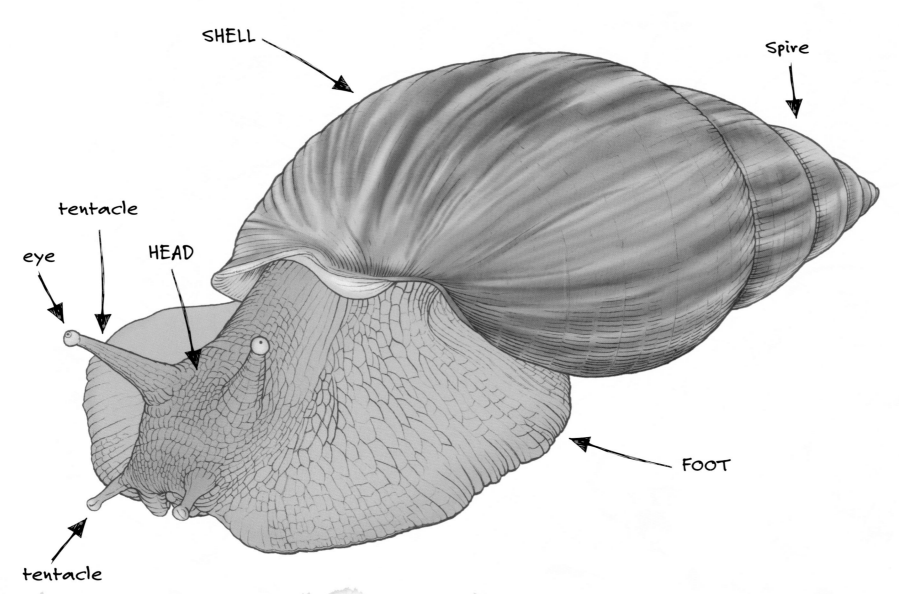

SHELL

Spire

tentacle

eye

HEAD

tentacle

FOOT

HOW DO GIANT LAND SNAILS FEED?

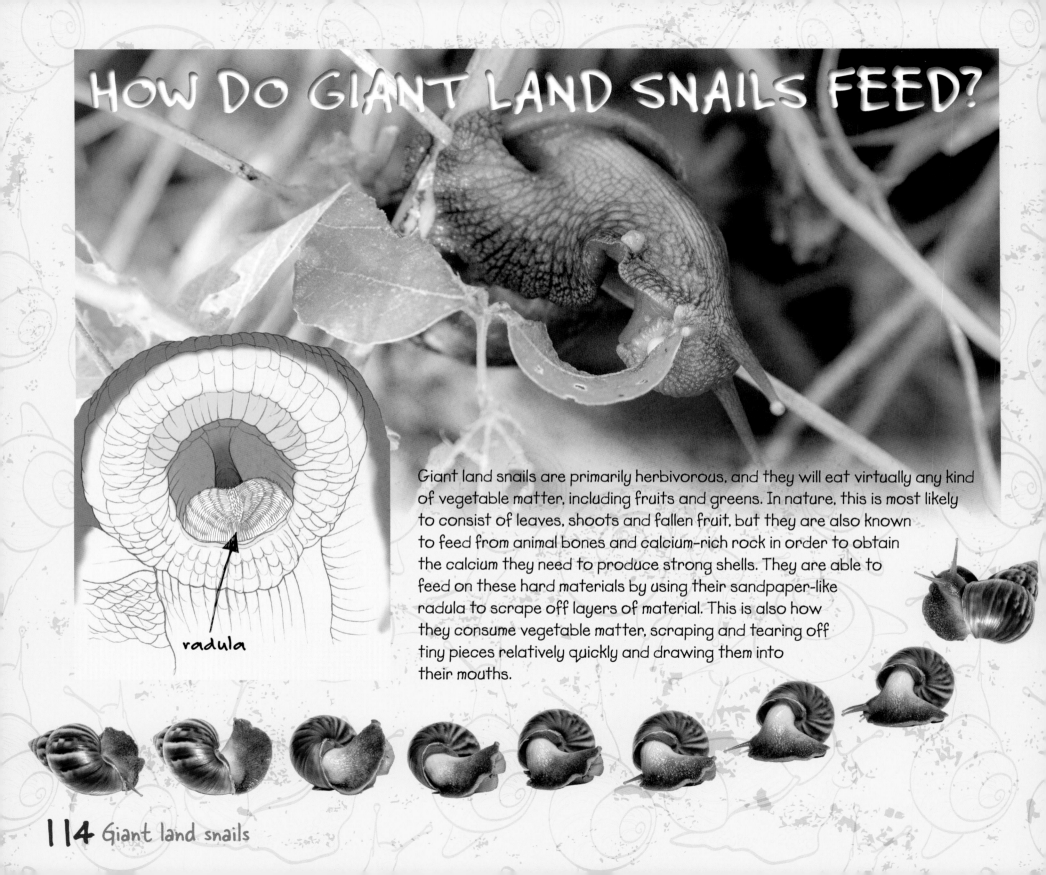

radula

Giant land snails are primarily herbivorous, and they will eat virtually any kind of vegetable matter, including fruits and greens. In nature, this is most likely to consist of leaves, shoots and fallen fruit, but they are also known to feed from animal bones and calcium-rich rock in order to obtain the calcium they need to produce strong shells. They are able to feed on these hard materials by using their sandpaper-like radula to scrape off layers of material. This is also how they consume vegetable matter, scraping and tearing off tiny pieces relatively quickly and drawing them into their mouths.

EYE SPY!

Many snails are nocturnal and do not rely on complex eyes to find their way around in the night. Some have eyes that consist only of light-sensitive cells that allow them to tell the difference between light and dark. Others have cup-shaped pits filled with light-sensitive cells that give them basic vision. Others, like the giant land snails, have a more developed eye that includes a lens and transparent, protective cornea, allowing them to see quite well. But that's not all. Each of their eyes contains an extra eye with its own smaller lens and light-sensitive cells. It is thought that these extra eyes detect changes in light even when the snail's eye-tentacles have been pulled in defensively, possibly helping them to guess when predators have moved away.

DEFENCE BEHAVIOUR

Snails carry protective shells on their backs, and this is the primary means of defence. When threatened, snails usually retract into their shells until danger passes. A snail will also pull its eye tentacles into its body when touched, to protect the eyes from damage.

WHERE ARE GIANT LAND SNAILS FOUND?

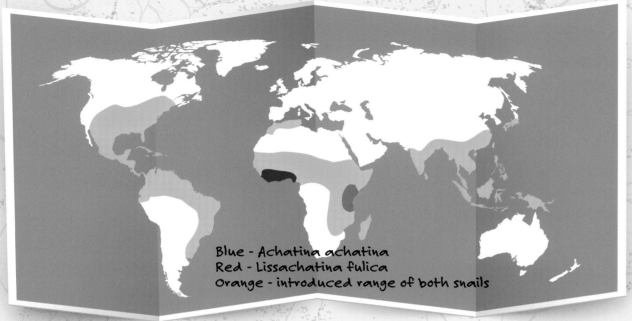

Blue - Achatina achatina
Red - Lissachatina fulica
Orange - introduced range of both snails

African giant land snails are found across tropical Africa, mainly in the west (from Sierra Leone east to Cameroon) and the east (Kenya, Tanzania and Mozambique). They are invasive across Southeast Asia, southern China, the USA and the West Indies.

WATER PRESSURE

The tentacles bearing the eyes and smelling organs of snails are controlled by muscles which can pull them in away from danger. However, they cannot push them back out. Instead, other muscles squeeze fluid into the tentacles, forcing them back out using water pressure!

LIFE CYCLE OF A GIANT LAND SNAIL

Giant land snails may lay clutches of 50–400 eggs at a time every few months. Once laid, the eggs take 12–15 days to hatch, giving rise to perfect miniatures of the adult snails. The young are just a few millimetres long and usually start to feed within a few days of being hatched (although sometimes they don't start eating for up to a week). Once they start eating, they feed heavily and increase in size rapidly, reaching sexual maturity at the age of about one to two years, depending on the species, if conditions are warm and food plentiful. Sexual maturity can be reached when the snails are just 8–10cm long, and once maturity is reached, growth slows. Even so, the snails will continue to increase in size for their entire lives. Given that giant land snails will, in general, live for 6–10 years if well looked after, their shell can be as long as 20cm, sometimes even more. The largest specimens are recorded from the wild, where conditions are optimal for much of the year.

Giant land snails are hermaphrodites, which means that each individual has male and female sex organs. Even so, self-fertilisation is uncommon, and reproduction normally requires two adult snails. When the animals are of similar size, sperm is passed in both directions by each of the animals, but when one is larger, the larger snail usually plays the role of the female. In that case, the smaller snail will pass its male sex cells to the larger snail to fertilise the eggs that it produces.

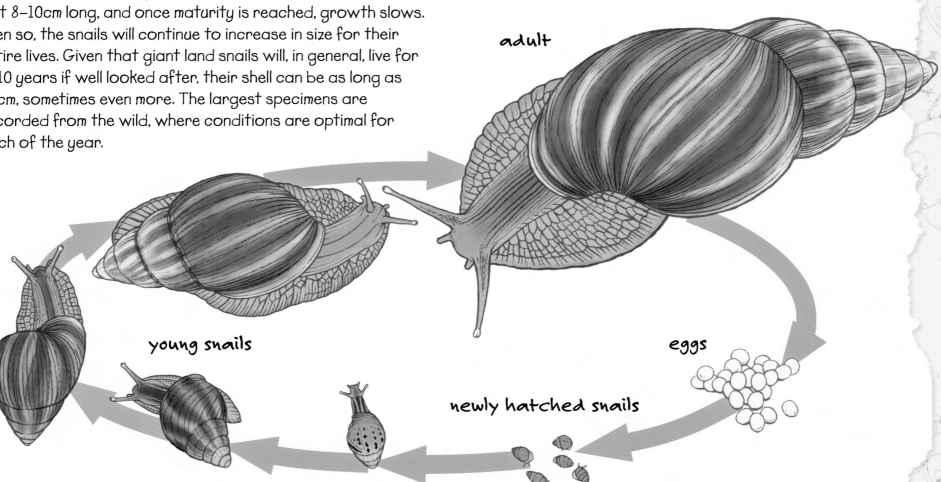

adult

young snails

newly hatched snails

eggs

TYPES OF GIANT LAND SNAILS

Approximately 35,000 species of snails adapted to life away from water and are known as land snails, as opposed to sea snails and freshwater snails. Of this total, a few hundred species are regarded as 'giants' (growing 20cm in length or more). Many giant land snail species are in captivity, but the overwhelming majority belong to just two species: the Giant African Land Snail (*Lissachatina fulica*) and the Giant Tiger Land Snail (*Achatina achatina*).

By far the most common is the **GIANT AFRICAN LAND SNAIL** (*Lissachatina fulica*, also known as *Achatina fulica*), and if a supplier does not specifically identify the type of snail they are selling, it is usually this species. The Giant African Land Snail is East African, hailing mainly from Kenya and Tanzania, but found in adjacent countries and now spread and naturalised in West Africa. This species, which is the easiest to keep, generally attains sizes of about 12cm long and 6cm wide, rarely becoming as large as 20cm.

The **GIANT TIGER LAND SNAIL** (*Achatina achatina*) is mainly found along a long coastal band that runs from Sierra Leone through Ghana to Cameroon, and 100–300km inland. Adults are typically 15–20cm long and up to 10cm wide. This species is slower growing, maturing at two to three years old in the wild, and can be harder to raise. In captivity, maturity can be achieved more quickly if conditions and feeding are optimal. Specimens up to 30cm long and 20cm wide have been documented and make this species the largest species of land snail alive today. Large specimens are not often encountered in captivity, except where conditions are perfect.

It can be very difficult to distinguish between the two species without expert advice.

HOW TO KEEP A GIANT LAND SNAIL

Provided you can keep them warm, giant land snails are relatively easy to look after with simple equipment. To keep a giant land snail, you need the following:

1 A plastic or glass enclosure about 40cm long, 30cm wide and 30cm tall is ideal for two adult giant land snails. The enclosure must have a securely fitting lid with ventilation

2 Peat-free potting soil or moss for the bottom of the tank – never use sand

3 Hiding places, such as pieces of bark, upturned pots, etc.

4 A sturdy plastic water dish

5 A spray bottle

6 A heating pad with a thermostat to control temperatures

7 Fresh fruit and vegetables

8 A calcium source, such as cuttlefish bone.

Suitable enclosures

Fish tanks made of glass or plastic are ideal, but they must have ample ventilation by way of a secure mesh or plastic-grille top that cannot be pushed off. Snails are very strong, so it is important that the lid is secure. Since they respond to light, the tank walls should be transparent rather than opaque, making plastic buckets unsuitable except during cleaning.

The bottom of the tank should be filled to a depth of 6–8cm with potting soil or similar material. Do not use soil from local woodlands. Porous substrates like soil help to retain moisture and increase humidity, which is very important for these tropical animals, humidity of about 80% being ideal.

The substrate should always be kept damp, and this can be achieved by spraying it with water in the morning and the evening. The soil should never be wet, nor should it be allowed to dry out. Placing a small dish of water in one corner will help maintain sufficiently high levels of humidity.

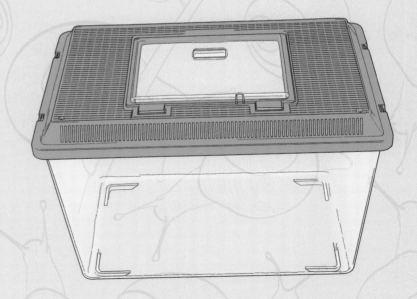

A suitable enclosure for keeping a giant land snail

Other requirements

Giant land snails benefit from constant conditions, with only small swings in temperature from day to night. A range of 18–30°C is acceptable, however giant snails do best at 23–26°C, and maintaining a constant temperature in this range is ideal. This is relatively close to room temperature in many houses, but if you live somewhere with cool weather you can use a thermostatically controlled heat pad pressed against one side of the enclosure. If you use a heater, make sure the soil never completely dries out as the additional warmth with speed up evaporation.

Including pieces of 'furniture' such as slabs of bark, branches or pots will provide your snails with places to explore and hide. However, it is best to avoid ceramic pots as these may damage your snails should they fall from the top of the tank – plastics can be a little more forgiving!

Setting up a giant land snail enclosure

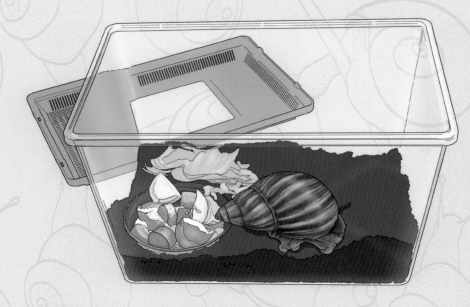

A fully set up giant land snail enclosure

The enclosures of giant land snails should be kept clean to avoid disease and ill health. This includes removing all uneaten food after a few hours (particularly soft fruit). The substrate should be inspected and waste material removed. It should also be substituted bit by bit to remove other accumulated waste. Once a month, the enclosure should be emptied and rinsed with very hot water, the sides cleaned of all dirt (do not use soap), dried with a paper towel and the living environment set up again.

It is important to check the substrate of mature snails a few times a week for buried eggs. Unless breeding snails, you may be required by law to destroy the eggs – certainly, they must not be simply thrown in the rubbish without either breaking them or pouring boiling water over them in a bowl. This may seem cruel, but these snails may lay over 1,000 eggs per year and it is simply impossible to raise or give away all of these potential new snails. Moreover, it is illegal to release the young as they are an environmental pest and may destroy native plants, introduce new diseases to the environment and endanger local wildlife. If destroyed early on, the eggs will have hardly developed.

Feeding your giant land snail

Giant land snails can eat virtually any fruit or vegetable consumed by humans, provided they are free of harmful chemicals and pesticides. Vegetables such as broccoli, cabbage, carrot, courgette, beans, potatoes and kale are all excellent, while fruits might include apples, bananas, pumpkin, papaya, pear, strawberries and tomatoes. The snails will also consume small amounts of raw minced meat, which can provide valuable protein. However, this should not be left to spoil. It is also important to provide a lime source in the form of a cuttlefish bone or egg shells. Cuttlefish bones are available from many pet stores, or online – always make sure that they have been washed free of salt if not provided by a pet supplier. A shallow dish of water will keep humidity high and allow them to drink or bathe if they wish to do so.

Holding your giant land snail

Giant land snails are easy to handle and are not particularly stressed by being picked up. Always wash your hands thoroughly before and after handling them – this protects them from any chemicals that might be on your hands, including moisturisers, soaps, perfumes, etc., all of which can irritate their skin.

When your hands are clean, spray them with water. If the snail is on the substrate, simply grasp the snail gently by its shell and place it onto your other hand, where it can be allowed to explore. If it is attached to the side of the enclosure, gently grasp it by the shell and then slide a wet finger on your other hand, under its head and run it along the length of its body to get it to detach. Never pull it away from the enclosure wall forcefully! Always be careful not to drop snails as a fall can smash their shells. For this reason it is best to handle them over a tabletop or a carpeted surface. Also avoid pickup up a snail by putting pressure on the sides of the shell next to the opening, as these parts of the snail can be thin and brittle (especially in young snails).

Always thoroughly wash your hands after you have finished handling the snail.

Breeding giant land snails

Single giant land snails can self-fertilise, but usually it takes two individuals to produce eggs (see life cycle, page 117). Eggs are normally buried in the substrate and will need to be unearthed. If you want to raise more snails, select just a few eggs and leave them where they are before removing and destroying the remainder.

The eggs will develop quickly and usually hatch within two or three weeks. The young will emerge to the surface on their own a few days after they hatch. They usually start eating within a few days, but some many not eat for up to a week. Young snails will eat the same foods as adults. It is easiest to monitor them by moving them to a smaller plastic container with a ventilated lid and substrate. This can simply be placed in the main enclosure, the lid preventing the adults from entering and possibly smothering the young. The young are very delicate and should not be picked up before they are 1cm long. Allow them to climb onto their food and simply transfer that to their nursery container!

CUTE SLIMY SNAIL BABIES!

Unlike many other invertebrates, giant African land snails do not have a larval form, but emerge from their eggs as perfect and exact miniatures of adult snails! They eat the same foods as adults, and grow very quickly!

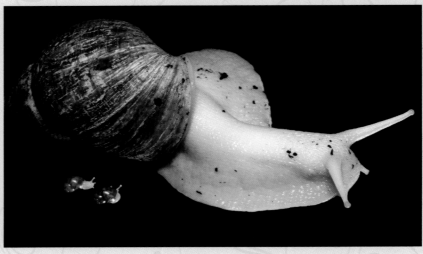

Suppliers

The following companies are recommended as ethical sources of livestock, enclosures, equipment and live food insects (e.g. crickets for feeding mantises).

Please remember: all pets are living creatures with specific needs. Read the Golden Rules on pages 8 to 9 and think really carefully about the conditions you can provide before purchasing any animal.

Bugzarre – www.bugzarre.co.uk
Supplier of cages and equipment, as well as beetle food jelly.

BugzUK – www.bugzuk.com
Supplier of a wide range of invertebrates, books and equipment.

Livefoods Direct – www.livefoodsdirect.co.uk
Supplier of crickets and other live food.

Martin Goss – www.martingoss.co.uk
Supplier of invertebrates and equipment.

Metamorphosis – www.metabugs.co.uk
Supplier of wide range of invertebrates, equipment, and a wonderful travelling insectarium for schools and birthdays.

Small-Life Supplies – www.small-life.co.uk
Supplier of insects, books and equipment.

Stratford-upon-Avon Butterfly Farm – www.butterflyfarm.co.uk
A butterfly farm with a wide range of pupae for sale.

Virginia Cheeseman – www.virginiacheeseman.co.uk
Supplier of a wide range of invertebrates and equipment.

Worldwide Butterflies – www.wwb.co.uk
Supplier of a wide range of butterfly and moth eggs, larvae and pupae. Including artificial silkworm food enabling rearing silkworms without mulberry leaves.

Societies and organisations

The following offer wonderful resources for learning more about invertebrates and their conservation. Many of the following societies have meetings, that offer lectures, livestock exchange opportunities and forums to meet and discuss with renowned expects.

Amateur Entomologist' Society: www.amentsoc.org

British Entomological and Natural History Society: www.benhs.org.uk

Buglife: www.buglife.org.uk

London Natural History Society: www.lnhs.org.uk

Phasmid Study Group: www.phasmidstudygroup.org

Royal Entomological Society: www.royensoc.co.uk

Many counties in the United Kingdom also have local entomological and nature societies. Check locally to see if your county does!

Entomological fairs

Entomological fairs are gatherings of suppliers, societies, experts and enthusiasts all centred around the world of insects. Attending an entomological fair is an amazing and eye-opening experience into the world of creepy crawlies!

There are up to 20 entomological fairs a year across the UK. Contact the societies or suppliers opposite for this year's dates. The largest ones are:

Midland Entomological Fayre

Biannual – usually April and December, www.midland-entomological-fayres.com

Amateur Entomologist' Society Annual Exhibition and Trade Fair

Usually October, www.amentsoc.org/events/exhibitions.html

International Herpetological Society

Multiple fairs, usually September and November, the focus is on reptiles, but features lots of invertebrates too. www.ihs-web.org.uk

Butterfly farms

Butterfly farms allow children up close and personal encounters with butterflies and moths, and often inspire enthusiasm for rearing insects at home. Some of the best butterfly farms in the UK include:

Butterfly Paradise – www.zsl.org
London Zoo, London

Butterfly House – www.zsl.org
Whipsnade Zoo, Whipsnade, near Dunstable

Butterfly World – www.butterfly-world.co.uk
Eaglescliffe, Stockton

Seaforde Gardens and Tropical Butterfly House – www.seafordegardens.com
Seaforde, County Down

Stratford Butterfly Farm – www.butterflyfarm.co.uk
Stratford-upon-Avon, Warwickshire

The Magic of Life Butterfly House – www.magicoflife.org
Aberystwyth, Ceredigion, Wales

Tropical Butterfly House – www.butterflyhouse.co.uk
Sheffield, South Yorkshire

Wye Valley Butterfly Zoo – www.butterflyzoo.co.uk
Ross-on-Wye, Herefordshire

Butterfly and moth counts

You can aid the work of conservationists by taking part in butterfly and moth counts in your local area. For more information visit the following websites.

www.bigbutterflycount.org

www.butterfly-conservation.org

www.mothscount.org

www.ukbms.org

Photographic credits

The publisher and author would like to thank all those photographers and image makers who have contributed to this book. All illustrations are credited to Marc Dando except those credited below.

Key: t = top; tl = top left; tr = top right; tc = top centre; c = centre; b = bottom; bl = bottom left; br = bottom right. IS = iStock; SS = Shutterstock.

2 Mathisa/SS; 5 br NUM LPPHOTO/SS; 6 Stewart McPherson; 7 tl Stewart McPherson, bl D. Kucharski K. Kucharska/SS, tr lcswart/SS, cr Protasov AN/SS, br Eric Isselee/SS; 9 Eric Isselee/SS; 10 Zety Akhzar/SS; 11 parilovv/123rf; 12 l Andrenko Tatiana/SS, c GParker/SS, tr Zety Akhzar/SS, br CJansuebsri/SS; 13 l HelloRF Zcool/SS, tr YoONSpY/SS, br Kletr/SS; 14 tl Sergiy Palamarchuk/SS, bl vanchai/SS, tr Jari Sokka/SS, background Artur Balytskyi/SS; 15 tl PISUTON'c/SS, tr Henrik Larsson/SS, br nujames10/SS, background Artur Balytskyi/SS; 16 l Eric Isselee/SS, tr Videowokart/SS, br Andrea Izzotti/SS, background EkaterinaP/SS; 17 l Matt9122/SS, cr Ethan Daniels/SS, br Kristina Vackova/SS, background EkaterinaP/SS; 18 l Eric Isselee /SS, r Marek Velechovsky/SS; 18–35 background Zvereva Yana/SS; 20 bl Devid Camerlynck/SS, tc schankz/SS, tr Maciej Olszewski/SS; 21 l eshoot/SS, r Cathy Keifer/SS; 22 b Eric Isselee/SS, r Pairoj Sroyngern/SS; 24 l CRS PHOTO/SS, r saodaeng/SS; 25 tl OlegD/SS, bl MF Photo/SS, r davemhuntphotography/SS; 26 tl kurt_G/SS, bl CathyKeifer/123RF, r Alen thien; 27 l Eric Isselee/SS, tr Ondrej Prosicky/SS, br John Cancalosi/naturepl.com; 28 tl Arif Supriyadi/SS, bl AlexIky/SS, r Cathy Keifer/SS; 29 tl Hue Chee Kong/SS, bl Vince Adam/SS, c Chayawitt Pooranapong/SS, r AsepBachowie; 30 l Kingcraft/SS; 31 r Serg Salivon/SS; 32 tr Guillermo Guerao Serra/SS, br Dan Olsen/SS; 33 l YoONSpY/SS, r Dusit Wongwattanakul/SS; 34 l chinahbzyg/SS, tr & br Eric Isselee/SS; 35 r Jiri Prochazka/SS; 36–53 background hchjjl/SS; 36 l kamnuan/SS, r Geza Farkas/SS; 38 tl Guillermo Guerao Serra/SS, bl itsmejust/SS, tr Oh suti/SS, br D. Kucharski K. Kucharska/SS; 39 l & br Eric Isselee/SS, tr nature production/naturepl.com; 40 tl kurt_G/SS, cl muhamad mizan bin ngateni/SS, bl jaiman taip/SS; 41 all Eric Isselee/SS; 42 l Ava Peattie/SS, tr Martin Veleta/SS, br Guillermo Guerao Serra/SS; 43 l Aedka Studio/SS, r Salparadis/SS; 44 Guillermo Guerao Serra/SS; 45 l fntproject/SS, r Martin Veleta/SS; 46 l Dr Morley Read/SS, r Aleksey Stemmer/SS; 47 SS; 48 sirtravelalot/SS; 50 PeingjaiChiangmai/SS; 51 l Guillermo Guerao Serra/SS, tr Ratchanee Sawasdijira/SS, br Stewart mcpherson; 52 t Dan Olsen/SS, b zaidi razak/SS; 53 tl Volkov Alexey/SS, bl Guillermo Guerao Serra/SS, r Stewart McPherson; 54–76 backgrounds geraria/SS, Curly Pat/SS; 54 tl Marco Uliana/SS, bl Tatevosian Yana/SS, tr CyberKat/SS; 56 tl IrinaK/SS, bl Cornel Constantin/SS, tr Mathisa/SS, br Christian Musat; 57 l Gorawut Thuanmuang, tr Joab Souza/SS, br yod67/SS; 58 t Agatha Kadar/SS, tr Mike Beauregard (CC BY 2.0), tr Cornel Constantin/SS, br Savo Ilic/SS; 59 r Matee Nuserm/SS; 60 l Ksenia Ragozina/SS, tr Calin Tatu/SS, br PRILL/SS; 61 tl Sandra Standbridge/SS, bl DJTaylor/SS, tr Leighton Photography & Imaging/SS, br Zeynur Babayev/SS; 62 tl HHelene/SS, bl Cheryl Thomas/SS, tr rorue/SS, br Przemyslaw Muszynski/SS; 63 tl Matyas Rehak/SS, bl Cosmin Manci/SS, tr mssy/SS, br Matee Nuserm/SS; 64 tl Lukas Gojda/SS, bl Matt Jeppson/SS, tr RudiErnst, br Rita Szilvasi/SS; 65 tl Ondrej Prosicky/SS, bl Tim Zurowski/SS, tr & br Matee Nuserm/SS; 66 tl SailsKool/SS, bl neil hardwick/SS, tr thelittleflower/SS, br Lori Martin/SS; 67 tl Jussi Lindberg/SS, bl Milan Zygmunt/SS, tl Bildagentur Zoonar GmbH/SS, bl thatmacroguy/SS; 68 tl ajt/SS, bl neil hardwick, tl Chekaramit/SS, bl Henri Koskinen/SS; 69 tl Robert Garner/SS, bl neil hardwick/SS, tr & br Protasov AN/SS; 70 tl Steven R Smith/SS, bl neil hardwick/SS, tr Matt Jeppson/SS, br Matt Jeppson/SS; 71 tl Andreas Weitzmann/SS, bl Kosol Aiyararat/SS, tr Andreas Weitzmann/SS, br Matt Jeppson/SS; 72 l A3pfamily/SS; 73 r Sandra Standbridge/SS; 74 t paulcreative/SS, br SanderMeertinsPhotography/SS; 75 tl Henri Koskinen/SS, bl Matt Jeppson/SS; 76 tl Mathisa/SS, bl & bc neil hardwick/SS, tr Mathisa/SS, br Thammanoon Khamchalee/SS; 77 tl Le Do/SS, bl Breck P. Kent/SS, bc Sari ONeal/SS, br Cathy Keifer/SS; 78–91 backgrounds Mart/SS; 78 l Siyanight/SS, r andrewshap15/SS; 79 bl Protasov AN/SS; 80 bl MongPro/SS, t Suede Chen/SS, br Henrik Larsson/SS; 81 bl PhimSri/SS, tr Protasov AN/SS, br Cosmin Manci/SS; 82 bl Dirk Ercken/SS, tr Pan Xunbin/SS; 84 tl Dmitri Gomon/SS, tr D. Kucharski K. Kucharska/SS, br Guillermo Guerao Serra/SS; 85 tl Milan Zygmunt, bl Guillermo Guerao Serra/SS, tr Aleksey Stemmer/SS; 86 tl Marek R. Swadzba/SS, tr feathercollector/SS; 87 tl Purino/SS; 88 tl Martin Fowler/SS; 89 tl Guillermo Guerao Serra/SS, tr mutsu7211/SS, br Dmitri Gomon/SS; 90 tl gorosan/SS, bl Balakleypb/SS, br Guillermo Guerao Serra/SS; 91 tl Tanawat Palee/SS, tr BLUR LIFE 1975/SS, br Jiri Prochazka/SS; 92 l davemhuntphotography /SS, tr TOSDY 1997/SS, br Butterfly Hunter/SS; 93–103 background hchjjl/SS; 94 bl mr. teerapon tiuekhom/SS, tr Cornel Constantin/SS; 95 ct ManutC/SS, cc lovelyday12/SS, b (main) Nonot/SS, tr Bankrx/SS, cr Suppavut Varutbangkul/SS; 96 bl asawinimages/SS, r Tim Bertelink (CC BY-SA 4.0).; 97 r Dennis van de Water/SS; 98 l Piotr Naskrecki/Minden Pictures/FLPA, tr Marek Velechovsky/SS, br TOSDY 1997/SS, 99 tl Dan Olsen/SS, bl Dennis van de Water/SS, tr Tukkatar/SS, br SIMON SHIM/SS; 100 tl Stewart Mcpherson, bl kurt_G/SS, cr fivespots/SS, br kamnuan/SS; 101 tl BLUR LIFE 1975; 102 br Stewart Mcpherson, 103 tl Cocos.Bounty, br Mr.Prasit BOONMA; 104 l IrinaK/SS, r Jan Hamersky/naturepl.com; 106 l IrinaK/SS, r Dmitry Fch/SS; 107 l Catmando/SS, b Rise0011(CC BY-SA 3.0); 109 l Kim Taylor/naturepl.com; 110 tr alle/SS, br Stewart McPherson; 111 bl alle/SS, tr Dmitry Fch/SS; 112 l NinaM/SS, tr Bruce Ellis/SS; 113–123 background Goodreason/SS; 114 t Elton Abreu/SS, b Mathisa/SS; 115 l Eugene R; r Muhammad Naaim/SS; 116 bl Kadroman/SS, tr Anatoly Epifanov/SS; 118 l Volosh/SS, tr Mark Brandon/SS, br Pan_Da/SS; 119 l Janice Smith, tr Schneckenmama (CC BY 2.0 DE), br Vladislav T. Jirousek/SS; 120 tl nata-lunata/SS; 122 tl P.D.T.N.C/SS, b Rowena Millar, r Stewart McPherson; 123 l Albert Yarullin/SS, bl Svitlyk/SS, tr H1nksy/SS, br Dan Olsen/SS.

Backgrounds thoughout Lutya/SS, pictorexniks/SS. **Map bases:** Creative Mood/SS.

Cover front background Lutya/SS, l Johnny Melack/SS, tr irin717/istock, br panor156/SS.
Cover back background Lutya/SS, bl Eric Isselee/SS, tr Mikhail Stepanov/123RF.

About the author

Stewart McPherson is a British naturalist, author and film-maker. Fascinated by wildlife from an early age, he began writing his first book at the age of sixteen. Stewart went on to study geography at the University of Durham. On graduating, he spent ten years climbing 300 mountains across the world (some of which were previously unexplored), to study and photograph carnivorous plants in the wild. Along the way, he co-discovered and co-named 35 new species/varieties of carnivorous plants, including some of the largest pitcher plants ever discovered and wrote a series of 25 books.

After featuring in short sequences in several broadcast documentaries, Stewart and a camera team travelled to all of the UK Overseas Territories to document the wildlife, cultures, history and landscapes that the territories harbour. This journey took three years to complete, and the resulting documentary series was released as *Britain's Treasure Islands* on the BBC, National Geographic, SBS and many other channels. The accompanying *Britain's Treasure Islands* book was distributed across the UK, and (through sponsorship) were donated to 5,350 secondary schools and 2,000 libraries.

Stewart wrote this Amazing Pets book and made 14 accompanying online films because he believes rearing small invertebrates at home and in schools is a powerful way for young people to be awed by the metamorphosis of a butterfly or the intricate beauty of a leaf insect. He hopes that if children experience nature up close and personal, tomorrows naturalists and conservationists may be nurtured and inspired. Stewart remains extremely grateful to the Don Hanson Charitable Foundation for sponsoring the donation of one copy of this work to each of 10,000 primary schools across the UK!

RHS Spectacular Plants

If you have enjoyed this book and would like to get more involved with nature, we have this accompanying title just for you. For more about this title visit our website at

www.wildnaturepress.com

Spectacular plant films online

Visit www.weirdandwonderfulpets.com to see 14 videos made by Stewart McPherson exploring the world's most incredible plant species and how to grow them. Hundreds of photographs, key growing advice and further resources are also available at this website.

Recommended species index